D0384473

T2-CBH

David "Dav" Pilkey

WHO WROTE THAT?

LOUISA MAY ALCOTT
JANE AUSTEN
AVI
L. FRANK BAUM
JUDY BLUME, SECOND EDITION
BETSY BYARS
MEG CABOT
BEVERLY CLEARY
ROBERT CORMIER
BRUCE COVILLE
ROALD DAHL
CHARLES DICKENS
ERNEST J. GAINES
THEODOR GEISEL
S.E. HINTON
WILL HOBBS
ANTHONY HOROWITZ
STEPHEN KING
MADELEINE L'ENGLE
GAIL CARSON LEVINE
C.S. LEWIS
LOIS LOWRY
ANN M. MARTIN
STEPHENIE MEYER
L.M. MONTGOMERY
PAT MORA
WALTER DEAN MYERS
ANDRE NORTON
SCOTT O'DELL
BARBARA PARK
KATHERINE PATERSON
GARY PAULSEN
RICHARD PECK
TAMORA PIERCE
DAVID "DAV" PILKEY
EDGAR ALLAN POE
BEATRIX POTTER
PHILIP PULLMAN
MYTHMAKER: THE STORY OF J.K. ROWLING, SECOND EDITION
MAURICE SENDAK
SHEL SILVERSTEIN
GARY SOTO
JERRY SPINELLI
R.L. STINE
EDWARD L. STRATEMEYER
E.B. WHITE
LAURA INGALLS WILDER
LAURENCE YEP
JANE YOLEN

David "Dav" Pilkey

Dennis Abrams

Foreword by
Kyle Zimmer

David "Dav" Pilkey

Chelsea House
An imprint of Infobase Publishing
132 West 31st Street
New York, NY 10001

Library of Congress Cataloging-in-Publication Data
Abrams, Dennis, 1960-
David "Dav" Pilkey / Dennis Abrams.
p. cm. — (Who wrote that?)
Includes bibliographical references and index.
ISBN 978-1-60413-500-8 (hardcover: acid-free paper) 1. Pilkey, Dav, 1966— Juvenile literature. 2. Authors, American—20th century—Biography—Juvenile literature. 3. Children's stories—Authorship—Juvenile literature. I. Title. II. Series.
PS3566.I51115Z52 2010
813'.54—dc22
[B] 2009022339

Chelsea House books are available at special discounts when purchased in bulk quantities for business, associations, institutions, or sales promotions. Please call our Special Sales Department in New York at (212) 967-8800 or (800) 322-8755.

You can find Chelsea House on the World Wide Web at http://www.chelseahouse.com

Text design by Keith Trego
Cover design by Alicia Post
Composition by EJB Publishing Services
Cover printed by Bang Printing, Brainerd, MN
Book printed and bound by Bang Printing, Brainerd, MN
Date printed: May 2010
Printed in the United States of America

10 9 8 7 6 5 4 3 2 1

This book is printed on acid-free paper.

Table of Contents

FOREWORD BY
KYLE ZIMMER
PRESIDENT, FIRST BOOK

HUMANITY IS POWERED by stories. From our earliest days as thinking beings, we employed every available tool to tell each other stories. We danced, drew pictures on the walls of our caves, spoke, and sang. All of this extraordinary effort was designed to entertain, recount the news of the day, explain natural occurrences—and then gradually to build religious and cultural traditions and establish the common bonds and continuity that eventually formed civilizations. Stories are the most powerful force in the universe; they are the primary element that has distinguished our evolutionary path.

Our love of the story has not diminished with time. Enormous segments of societies are devoted to the art of storytelling. Book sales in the United States alone topped $24 billion in 2006; movie studios spend fortunes to create and promote stories; and the news industry is more pervasive in its presence than ever before.

There is no mystery to our fascination. Great stories are magic. They can introduce us to new cultures, or remind us of the nobility and failures of our own, inspire us to greatness or scare us to death; but above all, stories provide human insight on a level that is unavailable through any other source. In fact, stories connect each of us to the rest of humanity not just in our own time, but also throughout history.

This special magic of books is the greatest treasure that we can hand down from generation to generation. In fact, that spark in a child that comes from books became the motivation for the creation of my organization, First Book, a national literacy program with a simple mission: to provide new books to the most disadvantaged children. At present, First Book has been at work in hundreds of communities for over a decade. Every year children in need receive millions of books through our organization and millions more are provided through dedicated literacy institutions across the United States and around the world. In addition, groups of people dedicate themselves tirelessly to working with children to share reading and stories in every imaginable setting from schools to the streets. Of course, this Herculean effort serves many important goals. Literacy translates to productivity and employability in life and many other valid and even essential elements. But at the heart of this movement are people who love stories, love to read, and want desperately to ensure that no one misses the wonderful possibilities that reading provides.

When thinking about the importance of books, there is an overwhelming urge to cite the literary devotion of great minds. Some have written of the magnitude of the importance of literature. Amy Lowell, an American poet, captured the concept when she said, "Books are more than books. They are the life, the very heart and core of ages past, the reason why men lived and worked and died, the essence and quintessence of their lives." Others have spoken of their personal obsession with books, as in Thomas Jefferson's simple statement: "I live for books." But more compelling, perhaps, is the almost instinctive excitement in children for books and stories.

Throughout my years at First Book, I have heard truly extraordinary stories about the power of books in the lives of children. In one case, a homeless child, who had been bounced from one location to another, later resurfaced—and the only possession that he had fought to keep was the book he was given as part of a First Book distribution months earlier. More recently, I met a child who, upon receiving the book he wanted, flashed a big smile and said, "This is my big chance!" These snapshots reveal the true power of books and stories to give hope and change lives.

As these children grow up and continue to develop their love of reading, they will owe a profound debt to those volunteers who reached out to them—a debt that they may repay by reaching out to spark the next generation of readers. But there is a greater debt owed by all of us—a debt to the storytellers, the authors, who have bound us together, inspired our leaders, fueled our civilizations, and helped us put our children to sleep with their heads full of images and ideas.

WHO WROTE THAT? is a series of books dedicated to introducing us to a few of these incredible individuals. While we have almost always honored stories, we have not uniformly honored storytellers. In fact, some of the most important authors have toiled in complete obscurity throughout their lives or have been openly persecuted for the uncomfortable truths that they have laid before us. When confronted with the magnitude of their written work or perhaps the daily grind of our own, we can forget that writers are people. They struggle through the same daily indignities and dental appointments, and they experience the intense joy and bottomless despair that many of us do. Yet somehow they rise above it all to deliver a powerful thread that connects us all. It is a rare honor to have the opportunity that these books provide to share the lives of these extraordinary people. Enjoy.

The humorous author and illustrator (and former class clown) Dav Pilkey likes to keep a low profile, believing his work should speak for itself. Pictured above, the cover of his book Captain Underpants and the Attack of the Talking Toilets.

1

Go Sit in the Hallway

WHEN YOU WERE YOUNGER, how often did you get in trouble at school? Did your teacher ever have to yell at you to get you to be quiet and stay quiet? Did you ever have to go sit out in the hallway until you *learned* to be quiet? Did you ever get sent to the principal? When Dav Pilkey was a kid, this happened almost every day.

It's not that he meant to be bad. He really didn't. But he just couldn't help himself. If there was a joke to be made, he made it. If there was a funny noise to be made, he was your guy. If there was a crayon to be shoved up his nose—well, he held the record for the number he could stick up there at one time. And although his classmates loved his antics, his teachers and the school principal felt somewhat differently about the matter. "I had a series of principals and teachers and people in my life . . . who were not very understanding of a kid who was kind of rambunctious and very, very silly, and they didn't like me very much and they were always trying to oppress me."[1] Indeed, young David Pilkey was so often "oppressed" that he set the school's record for the amount of time spent in the principal's office!

Eventually, the grown-ups discovered that David's misbehavior was not within his control. But before that happened, he found himself spending more and more time in the hallway. After a while, his teacher even set up a desk out there just for his exclusive use.

David learned to make the best of it. Every morning he would fill up his hallway desk with the items he would need for the day: paper, pencils, and crayons. That way, he was prepared when the teacher snapped her fingers, pointed at the door, and told him yet again to get out of her classroom.

MOTIVATION

Sometimes something that is meant to be a punishment is actually a blessing in disguise. It was during this solitary time, away from his friends, that David had the opportunity to use his carefully stashed art supplies. He began, as most artists do, by simply drawing pictures. As time went on, he began making up stories to go along with the pictures. Some of the stories involved superheroes. These powerful characters could do things that David could never do.

One character in particular seemed to leap off the page and stand out, both to David and his friends. Later he thanked his second grade teacher for the inspiration:

> My teacher actually inspired it, my second grade teacher. I had a lot of problems with her. No, no, she had a lot of problems with me, was the way it went, but one time she used the word "underpants" in a sentence, and I don't exactly remember what she said, but she said underpants, and everybody in the classroom just burst out laughing, and then she got really mad, and she's like "Boys and girls, underwear is not funny," and then we just laughed, you know so much harder at that, and it was at that moment that I realized, you know, "Underwear is a very powerful thing. Not only does it make everybody in my classroom laugh, but it makes my teacher really angry," you know, and that's sort of where Captain Underpants came from. I think, you know, within a few days I had created Captain Underpants and I was writing comics about him.[2]

History has proven the teacher wrong: apparently, underwear and the word "underpants" *are* funny. Decades after seven-year-old David Pilkey came up with the idea, there are more than 38 million copies of the adventures of Captain Underpants in print, making it one of the best-selling children's book series of all time.

Pilkey uses broad humor and parodies of art, literature, and popular culture in an effort to make reluctant readers *want* to read. Anything is fair game to him, including monster movies, superheroes, modern art, and science fiction. Pilkey's books target everything in their path. He makes readers laugh uproariously while delivering a message of friendship, tolerance, and the triumph of the good-hearted. Pilkey is one of the most popular and beloved authors of our time. He is the author of more than 50 books for children. These include the Dragon series, the Big Dog and Little Dog series, the Ricky Ricotta series,

Did you know...

Dav Pilkey is not the only person who had difficulties in school and went on to achieve great success as an adult. Many original thinkers, writers, and artists have felt straitjacketed in a formal, structured school system.

The famous French chemist and microbiologist Louis Pasteur, best known today for inventing the process for pasteurizing milk, was only a mediocre student. Charles Darwin, who developed the theories of natural selection and evolution, was told by his father, "You care for nothing but shooting, dogs, and rat-catching; you will be a disgrace to yourself and your family." Carl Jung, the influential psychologist, was considered by his teachers to be simply stupid. Even Albert Einstein, the twentieth century's greatest physicist, was expelled from school and was unable to gain admittance to the Zurich Polytechnic Institute!

The father of famed French sculptor Auguste Rodin, who is best known for his statue *The Thinker*, once said, "I have an idiot for a son." In fact, Rodin failed to earn admittance to the school of art three times. French author Émile Zola flunked literature. Even Leo Tolstoy, author of two of the greatest novels in world literature, *War and Peace* and *Anna Karenina*, was described as "both unable and unwilling to learn."

Source: R.S. Illingsworth and C.M. Illingsworth, *Lessons from Childhood: Some Aspects of Early Life of Unusual Men and Women* (Baltimore: William and Wilkins Co., 1966).

The celebrated twentieth-century physicist Albert Einstein, who won the Nobel Prize for Physics in 1921, was once described by one of his teachers as "mentally slow, unsociable, and adrift forever in his foolish dreams." Like Dav Pilkey, Einstein had trouble concentrating in school.

the Captain Underpants series, and numerous other stand-alone titles.

Of course, Pilkey's success has not been without controversy. As popular as the Captain Underpants books are with young readers, many parents, teachers, and librarians are appalled by the vulgarity, silliness, and nonstop toilet humor. Plots that revolve around the effects of dog breath and a school principal hypnotized into thinking he is a superhero who runs around in his underwear are unlikely to appeal to grown-ups looking for "safe" books for kids to read.

In an article written for the American Federation of Teachers' newsletter, a retired Texas schoolteacher argued that the books should not be included in elementary school reading:

> There is an incredible wealth of literature written for young people that is life affirming, humorous and fun to read. I do not include the writings of Dav Pilkey among them. His body of work is largely built on the lowest common denominator: the humor of bodily functions and frat-boy disrespect toward teachers, parents and adults in general.[3]

Others, of course, disagree. Many, like Sara Kelly Johns, argue that the Captain Underpants books get boys to read, opening the door for them to go on to read other books as well:

> It's about boys . . . boys learning to love reading and becoming lifelong readers. Boys choose books that are humorous and adventurous; getting one that captures their attention can be a trick. That's why school libraries may well have Captain Underpants on their shelves, at least for the few minutes

> between one boy returning a copy and another taking it out. School libraries have Captain Underpants books because they are fun and enticing and give elementary school librarians the opportunity to be magicians. They can wave the magic wand of books that will get students reading.[4]

Anne Hanson, school librarian at Hoover Elementary School in North Mankato, Minnesota, told Johns about the books and their author: "Dav Pilkey understands what it means to embrace silliness, even in a setting where it may be discouraged. We need silliness everywhere, but especially in the library where we want kids to understand what it means to read for pleasure. They love the adventure and the subversive elements of the heroes."[5]

It seems clear that Dav Pilkey, the best-selling author, is not all that different from young David Pilkey, the class clown who entertained his classmates while angering and annoying his teachers. How did he do it? How did the boy who was constantly in trouble find success as a writer? And, perhaps most important, how will Captain Underpants be able to fend off the attack of the talking toilets?

Shown from left are Moe Howard, Curly Howard, and Larry Fine, better known as The Three Stooges. This classic comedy team is one of Dav Pilkey's favorites. In fact, the Jerome Horwitz Elementary School in the Captain Underpants series was inspired by Curly's real name.

2

Normal Yet Different

IT IS IMPORTANT to understand that not all authors enjoy discussing their personal lives with their readers. Some share the details of their lives in interviews, articles, and speeches. Some hope that this will help their readers relate to them and to their books. Pilkey is not one of those writers. He dislikes doing interviews, avoids talking about his personal life, and is unwilling (with a few rare exceptions) to share his private life with his fans. But there a few topics that Pilkey is more than happy to talk about with his readers. These include his childhood difficulties, his beloved dogs, and his books.

"I WAS ALMOST ALWAYS HAPPY"

David Pilkey was born on March 4, 1966, in Cleveland, Ohio. His father, David M. Pilkey, was a sales manager for a steel company. His mother, Barbara, was a church organist. He has one sister, Cindy. According to her brother, Cindy had one great claim to fame: her amazing skill as a professional tattletale when they were young.

At that time, Cleveland was near its peak as an economic powerhouse. Located on the Cuyahoga River and Lake Erie, the city had long been a transportation center. When the Ohio and Erie Canal was completed in 1832, Cleveland was connected to the Atlantic Ocean via the Erie Canal and later via the St. Lawrence Seaway.

With easy transportation, businesses such as steel and automobile manufacturing moved in, eager to take advantage of inexpensive transportation costs. Major industries helped to boost the economy. The city became known as a center for the arts as well. The Cleveland Orchestra has long been regarded as one of the world's finest. During David and Cindy's childhood, Cleveland was considered one of the best places to live in the United States.

Dav Pilkey remembers almost always being happy as a child. His parents told him that he was so happy he would laugh in his sleep! And at a very early age he could usually be found drawing.

From the time he was old enough to hold a crayon or a pen, David loved to draw. It was not something he just wanted to do; it was something he *needed* to do. When the other kids on the block were outside playing baseball or football, he could be found in the house, drawing. He had a ready supply of countless sheets of drawing paper that his dad brought home from work. He eagerly filled them with

Did you know...

Like many young boys (and not a few young girls), young David Pilkey enjoyed watching The Three Stooges on television. The Stooges' short and feature-length films were often shown in the afternoon on school days or on Saturday mornings from the 1960s through the 1980s. But do you know who The Three Stooges were?

The Three Stooges were an American comedy act. They made dozens of films from the 1930s through the 1960s. Moe, Larry, and Curly was the earliest lineup of Stooges, followed by Moe, Larry, and Shemp; Moe, Larry and Joe; and finally Moe, Larry, and Curly Joe.

The hallmark of the Stooges, no matter who was in the lineup, was outrageous physical slapstick comedy. Typical antics included pies in the face, slaps in the face, and hair being pulled. The silly storylines were punctuated by fast-paced one-liners. For many fans, including Dav Pilkey, the greatest of the Stooges was Curly Howard, who, even today, is the most easily recognizable of them all, best known for his high-pitched voice, his vocal expressions ("nyuk-nyuk-nyuk" and "woo-woo-woo") as well as his physical comedy, comic improvisations, and sheer ability to take a fall.

How much does Pilkey love Curly? When he wrote his first Captain Underpants book, he named George and Harold's school after Curly—Jerome Horwitz Elementary School. Jerome Horwitz is Curly Howard's real name!

imaginative pictures of monsters, animals, and, of course, superheroes. David's parents encouraged him in his artistic endeavors and saved as much of his childhood work as they could. His early "Water Man" comics are posted on his Web site.

These early years were happy times, but, unfortunately for David, they weren't meant to last. He recalls on his Web site, "Life was pretty cool when I was little . . . and then school started."[1]

BAD TIMES

David Pilkey and his family were living in Elyria, Ohio, a city 23 miles southeast of Cleveland but considered to be part of the same greater metropolitan area, when David started going to St. John's Lutheran School. The strict teachers did not know what to do with young David Pilkey. He wanted to draw and make his friends laugh and he had difficulty concentrating in class. The teachers—and David—were not happy.

It was obvious that David had learning problems. He had difficulty paying attention and was labeled as being "severely hyperactive."[2] He had trouble reading, and, perhaps worst of all, he was unable to control his impulses, sit down quietly, and behave. In those early years in school, it often seemed to David that he was spending more time sitting in the hallway than in the classroom.

Today, he would be diagnosed with attention-deficit hyperactivity disorder, more commonly known as ADHD. You may know someone who has it and takes medicine to help them pay attention in class. The medications help to control a person's hyperactivity and lack of impulse control, two symptoms commonly associated with ADHD.

THE SCIENCE OF MISBEHAVIOR

ADHD is a neurobehavioral developmental disorder. What does that mean? Neurobehavioral means that by observing a person's behavior, one can assess any problems in their nervous system—the brain, spinal cord, and nerves. A developmental disorder is one that can interrupt normal development in children.

ADHD is said to affect about 3 to 5 percent of all children. About 2 million children in the United States have ADHD. So in a classroom of 25 to 30 children, it is likely that at least one child will have ADHD. Symptoms usually become apparent before a child is seven years of age. The most common symptoms of ADHD are:

1. Impulsiveness: acting before thinking of consequences, jumping from one activity to another, disorganized behavior, and a tendency to interrupt during conversations;
2. Hyperactivity: restlessness, an inability to sit still, fidgeting, squirminess, climbing on things, restless sleep;
3. Inattention: easily distracted, zoning out, not finishing work, difficulty listening.

Dr. Heinrich Hoffmann first described ADHD-like symptoms in 1845. Hoffmann was a German doctor who wrote books on medicine and psychiatry. He was also a poet, who became interested in writing for children when he was unable to find materials suitable to read to his three-year-old son. The result was a book of poems, complete with illustrations, about children and what they are like. His poem "The Story of Fidgety Philip" was an accurate description of a little boy with ADHD. When Hoffman wrote the poem, the syndrome that he described did not even have a name!

8. THE STORY OF FIDGETY PHILIP.

Let me see if Philip can
Be a little gentleman;
Let me see, if he is able
To sit still for once at table:
Thus Papa bade Phil behavè;
And Mamma look'd very grave.
But fidgety Phil,
He won't sit still;
He wriggles
And giggles,
And then, I declare,
Swings backwards and forwards
And tilts up his chair,
Just like any rocking horse; —
"Philip! I am getting cross!"

Heinrich Hoffmann, a German physician, wrote books on psychiatry, but became interested in writing for children when he was unable to find materials suitable to read to his three-year-old son. His poem "The Story of Fidgety Philip" was an accurate description of a little boy with all the symptoms of ADHD.

In 1902, Sir George F. Still published a series of lectures for the Royal College of Physicians in England in which he described a group of children with serious behavioral problems. He believed the behavior was caused by genetics and not by poor parenting. Today, these children would be diagnosed with ADHD.

Despite this early evidence, it was not until 1987 that ADHD was given its official designation in the American Psychiatric Association's *Diagnostic and Statistical Manual of Mental Disorders*. The causes of ADHD remain uncertain. Many studies suggest that genes, the basic biological units that determine the traits one inherits from one's family, play a large role. Like many other illnesses, ADHD is probably caused by a combination of factors. So in addition to genetics, researchers are looking at the possibility that environmental factors, brain injuries, nutrition, and social environment all might contribute to ADHD.

Before medication was available to treat ADHD, people tried to change the behavior of children with the disorder. This usually meant separating them from their peers and using firm discipline. This got kids to settle down temporarily, but it did not stop the symptoms. In the early 1960s, doctors started using a medicine called methylphenidate, best known by the brand name Ritalin, to treat ADHD. When David Pilkey was young, most people were not familiar with ADHD. So he was punished for something that he could not control.

Even today, Pilkey shudders at the thought of elementary school. "If I *could* go back? Ugh! I think I'd rather wait in line at the DMV [Department of Motor Vehicles] for 10 years."[3] But he would not change anything either. "Even though elementary school was a bad experience for me, I wouldn't change a thing. Who knows? If I'd had teachers who were kind and supportive and nurturing, I wouldn't have had anyone to rebel against, and I probably wouldn't have created Captain Underpants."[4]

It was a difficult time for David. He was unable to concentrate. He felt he was different from the other kids in his class and even just plain stupid. As an adult, Pilkey feels that it is important to tell people about his condition. "If I had known that people can grow up with these kinds of problems and still turn out OK," he says, "I might have had more hope. Once kids discover that you can still be successful in life even if you're not successful in school, I think they'll develop more confidence and hope."[5]

LAUGHTER AS A WEAPON

Unable to excel at academics, young David quickly established himself as the class clown. This proved to be his saving grace. By using humor, he was able to deflect his teacher's criticism and focus his energy on his consuming passion, drawing comic books. (Being the class clown did not mean he wasn't teased. Many of his former classmates still remember him as "David Puke-ey.")

David made homemade comics by stapling sheets of paper together and drawing by hand. He brought them to school and gave them to his friends. These were the comics that were the very beginning of Captain Underpants. Unfortunately, Pilkey no longer has any examples of these early works. He loaned many of them to friends who would "lose them, or spill stuff on them, and bring them back weeks later with pages missing and stuff."[6] Others were ripped up by his teachers. They would tell him to start taking life more seriously because, they said, he could not spend his life making silly books. (But, as Pilkey likes to point out, he was not a very good listener.)

School gradually got better for David, especially after reading became easier. Naturally, as the class clown, he always wanted to read "joke books" for his book reports. And, just as naturally, his teachers said "no." And since he could not find anything else he wanted to read, his teachers would, since he was boy, give him a book on sports and tell him to do his report on it. (Of course, since Pilkey hated sports as a kid, you can only imagine how he must have felt about those books!) But this all changed, as Pilkey explained years later:

> I first started enjoying books when our school began to work with Scholastic Book Clubs. Every month we'd get a little newsprint order form with lots of colorful pictures of books, and for some reason, those books seemed like *candy* to me. I'd spend *my own money* on books, believe it or not, and when the books got shipped to my classroom, I couldn't WAIT to start reading. And yes, all I ever bought were joke books and silly cartoon books . . . but look where it got me!
>
> I think that was the first time I discovered that reading could be fun, as long as I got to read what I wanted to read, and not what I was *supposed* to read.[7]

Of course, not all of David's teachers disapproved of him, and some offered him moral support. But his greatest sources of support and love were his parents. They did what they could to make him feel special. In an interview with *ADDitude Magazine*, he recalled:

> It was always so good to come home from school and be safe. They actually encouraged me to make comics, and would sit down and read each one when I was done. They always laughed in all the right places, and had good things to say about *MOST* of my stories (my folks were real conservative, so Captain Underpants' humor didn't really fly in our house).[8]

Not only did his parents support his love of drawing and telling stories, Pilkey gives his father credit for his sense of humor. "My dad was a bit of a pun-master. He's the one who came up with the name 'Hally-Tosis' for our dog, Hally, who had really bad breath. ('Hally-Tosis' sounds like the word 'halitosis,' which means 'bad breath.')"[9] Years later, Pilkey used this in a book called *Dog Breath*.

THINGS GET WORSE

High school was very difficult for David. His teachers, who did not understand his sense of humor or his art, tried to convince him to get serious. Like most kids his age, David was struggling to figure out what he wanted to do with his life. Two significant events during his high school years helped David to find his way.

The first of these events led to the new spelling of David's first name. In 1983, he was working as a waiter at a Pizza Hut restaurant. All the waiters wore nametags on their uniforms. When David's nametag was being made, the letter "e" on the label-maker broke. So instead of printing "Dave" it printed "Dav." Pilkey loved the new spelling and it stuck.

The second significant event might have been traumatic and discouraging for someone else. But not for Dav. His principal, who was fed up with his jokes and art and comic books, pulled him out of class one day. He said, "I know you think you're special because you can draw, but let me tell you something: artists are a dime a dozen. You will never make a living as an artist!"[10]

Instead of taking his principal's words to heart, Pilkey took them as a spur. He set out to prove the principal and everybody else wrong. Dav Pilkey was determined to show that he could use his art and sense of humor to make something of himself.

National Guardsmen fire a barrage of tear gas into a crowd of demonstrators on the campus of Kent State University on May 4, 1970. When the gas dissipated, four students lay dead and several others injured. Hundreds of students staged the demonstration in protest against the Nixon administration's expansion of the Vietnam War into Cambodia. Some years after these events, Dav Pilkey would attend a much more sedate Kent State, where he would be inspired to write for children.

3

Getting Discovered

IN 1984, DAV PILKEY entered Kent State University as a freshman, majoring in art. Having grown up in the Cleveland area, his choice of Kent State was a logical one: the school, located only 40 miles from his home in Cleveland, is one of America's largest university systems, with a fine reputation as a selective, traditional public research university. Founded in 1910 as the Kent State Normal School, a college for training public school teachers, the school was constructed on land donated by William S. Kent, the son of Marvin Kent, who was the namesake for the city of Kent. By 1915, the school's name had changed to Kent State Normal College and then Kent State College. It received full university status in 1935.

Sadly, the school is still most famously known for a violent Vietnam War protest. On May 4, 1970, a National Guard unit fired at unarmed students. Four students were killed and nine were wounded. The National Guard had been called into Kent after several protests over the United States' invasion of Cambodia during the Vietnam War had become violent, including rioting in downtown Kent and the burning of the school's ROTC (Reserve Officers Training Corps) building.

By the time Pilkey enrolled at Kent State, the Vietnam War was long over. He quickly settled into his new life at college. The more obvious symptoms of ADHD were under control, so he was able to concentrate on his classes. He made new friends and started to figure out what to do with his life.

Although he was maturing in many ways, Pilkey's irrepressible sense of humor had not changed much. He still enjoyed laughing at things that most adults considered silly. He loved making his friends and other classmates laugh. He held onto the part of him that was still a kid.

At college, Pilkey was encouraged by someone other than his parents to continue drawing and making up stories. His freshman English professor complimented him on his creative writing skills. Not only did he tell Pilkey that he thought he had talent, he encouraged him to *use* his talent to become a writer.

The idea hit Pilkey like a bolt out of the blue. He had always been the guy who could make his friends laugh with his imaginative stories and childlike sense of humor. It had never occurred to him that he could make a living doing this. Excited beyond belief, he realized that somehow, becoming a writer was what he had always wanted to do. Now, though, for the first time, someone was encouraging him to do make a career out of doing what he loved. It was a thrilling moment.

FIRST TASTE OF FAME

He immediately set to work improving his drawing and writing skills. Of course, Pilkey had other things in mind besides school and studying—dating in particular. And, interestingly enough, it was a girl who inspired his first book.

It was January 1986. Pilkey was trying to impress a girl that he was dating. He wrote and illustrated a book called *World War Won.* The book is set in the 1980s during the heated nuclear arms race between the Soviet Union and the United States. Two kings (a fox and a raccoon) get into a fight and try to frighten each other with their vast arsenals of weapons. Of course, since the author is Dav Pilkey, the weapons in question are not nuclear missiles. Instead, the two kings find themselves trapped on tall towers of laser potatoes, exploding cigars, and atomic tomatoes! Eventually, animal citizens of the two countries come together and end the threat of war once and for all.

Although the book may have impressed Pilkey's girlfriend, it was not enough to keep their relationship going. But the book had a huge impact on his life. One of his professors told him about a contest held by a publisher, Landmark Editions. The contest was called The National Written and Illustrated By . . . Award Contest for Students. People between the ages of six and 19 could submit a book they had written and illustrated. The winning book in each age group would be published by Landmark.

Nineteen-year-old aspiring writer Dav Pilkey mailed the first real book he had ever written to the contest and hoped for the best. Imagine his surprise when, just a few months later, he received a phone call from David Melton at Landmark Editions. Pilkey recalled:

> I'm not really sure what Mr. Melton said to me on the phone, I just remember hearing these three words: "you," "winner," and "congratulations." I think he talked for a while, but I have no idea what he said (or what I said for that matter). After that, all I remember was screaming and jumping up and down for about six months.[1]

Imagine what it must have felt like. For most of his life, Pilkey had felt stupid and out of place, told by teachers that he would never amount to anything. Now his very first attempt at writing a book was a contest winner. And the book was going to be published!

In December 1986, less than a year after he had started work on *World War Won*, he flew to Kansas City, Missouri. Pilkey recalls on his Web site:

> It was the most exciting time of my life. I'll never forget getting off the plane in Kansas City and meeting my new publisher for the first time. I tried to act normal, but I was *so* excited. It took every bit of self-control I had not to scream, jump up and down, and laugh hysterically . . . I was going to be an author![2]

There, at the offices of his new publisher, Pilkey worked with the staff to make his original manuscript into a published book. He designed the book's cover, worked with professional editors and art directors, and even saw the presses on which his book would be printed! It was a privilege few first-time authors experience.

Did you know...

When Dav Pilkey returned from his author tour promoting *World War Won*, he dated a young woman named Cynthia Rylant. She would go on to have a career as a respected author of fiction, nonfiction, and poetry for young adults.

Like Pilkey, Rylant had to overcome a difficult childhood in order to achieve her dreams. Born in Hopewell, Virginia, on June 6, 1954, she was just four years old when her parents divorced. She was sent to live with her grandparents in Cool Ridge, West Virginia. Her grandparents' house had no electricity or running water; and during the four years Cynthia lived there, she was unable to travel far from the house, since her grandparents did not own a car.

Growing up in a poor area of Appalachia, she was unsure of what she could do with her life after graduating from high school. Inspired by her mother's example, she decided to go to college. She attended what is now the University of Charleston. Later, she completed her master's degree in English at Marshall University. For a time, Rylant worked as a waitress. Then she got a job working in the children's section of the Akron Public Library. There she quickly found herself falling in love with children's literature.

Not yet planning to be a writer, she got another degree at Kent State University. There she met Pilkey. She soon began writing herself. Her first book for children, *When I Was Young in the Mountains*, received the American Book Award in 1982 and was a Caldecott Honor Book. Today, Rylant has written more than 100 books for children and young adults.

When *World War Won* was published in 1987, Pilkey had the opportunity to tour the country. He visited bookstores and schools to talk about the book. One fan still remembers Pilkey's visit to his school at the time:

> I was in fourth grade when this book came out, and Dav Pilkey came to visit my school. I loved it from the moment he began to read the first page. Not only is it hilariously entertaining and extremely clever, but it delivers an important message to today's children. As a political science major, I keep some of the book's closing thoughts at my desk to keep me grounded . . . "It's nice to have power and good to be strong, but threatening each other is certainly wrong. A powerful mind is good for a start, but you also need wisdom and love in your heart. And when you use all of these things as a guide, you can take your differences and lay them aside."[3]

While readers loved *World War Won*, reviewers had mixed feelings. In *School Library Journal*, Susan Scheps described the book as

> [A] charming group of deftly drawn cartoon animals [that] outshine the poetic text . . . A major flaw is Pilkey's effort to relate the story in poetic form. His attempt to rhyme and mete each couplet has resulted in excessive wordiness . . . [Still,] Pilkey's book provides a model for other young hopeful authors.[4]

After finishing his promotional tour, Pilkey returned to Kent State where he graduated in 1987 with an associate of arts degree. Unlike many graduates who leave college uncertain of their goals, Pilkey knew he was going to be a children's book writer. He realized that having his first book published may have been a lucky fluke. He could not depend on such breaks to make him a success. If he was going to be an author, he had to work hard and learn how to write.

The movie poster for Saps at Sea *(1940), featuring the legendary comedy duo of Stan Laurel and Oliver Hardy. Two of the turkeys in Dav Pilkey's book* 'Twas the Night Before Thanksgiving *are named after them.*

4

Learning How to Do It

ALTHOUGH HE WAS already a published author, Pilkey knew that he had to start at the beginning. Winning one contest did not, to his mind at least, mean that he knew what he was doing as a writer. The first book was a lucky break, something like hitting a home run the first time you picked up a baseball bat. And, just as no one is guaranteed another homer the next time at bat, Pilkey's next book might not be as good.

In order to become a successful children's book author, he had to study the world of children's literature. Writing children's books is more than just having a story to tell. You need to know *how* to tell the story: how to use words, sentences, and rhythms to capture the reader's attention and present the story effectively. Pilkey explained the process later:

> When I really got serious about writing children's books, I began reading everything I could by my favorite writers, Arnold Lobel, Cynthia Rylant, James Marshall, and Harry Allard. I read *Frog and Toad*, *Henry and Mudge*, *George and Martha*, and *The Stupids* over and over again, until I started to pick up rhythms and recognize patterns. Soon I began to see what really *worked* in these books—what made them great pieces of literature.[1]

Writing was something that Pilkey had to work hard to learn, but illustrating came easier. Even his earliest drawings—from broadly drawn cartoons in eye-poppingly bright colors to richly detailed paintings in more subtle colors and shades—showed that his talent was obvious. He worked in a variety of mediums, including watercolor, colored pencil, acrylics, magic markers, collage, and even, at least according to the artist himself, Hamburger Helper and Dijon mustard!

Pilkey's art is often inspired by popular culture, but also includes references to paintings of famous artists, such as Leonardo da Vinci, Vincent van Gogh, James McNeill Whistler, Grant Wood, and Edward Hopper. Some of his favorite artists are Pablo Picasso, Henri Rousseau, Joan Miro, and Marc Chagall—an impressive list of influences for someone best known for his irreverent attitude and "potty" humor.

PUTTING IT ALL TOGETHER

Feeling confident that he knew what he was doing, it was time for Pilkey to begin work on his second book. But what would he write about? He struggled for a while to come up

Did you know...

When Dav Pilkey began to research how to write a successful children's book, he did more than just read children's literature. He also thought about the kind of books that he liked as a kid. After all, he thought, if they could hold his attention, they would probably do the same for other kids.

He ended up with a list of rules that he swore he would try to follow when he wrote for children:

1. Books had to feature large type, not small type. Larger typeface means fewer words to read, so the book is less intimidating to reluctant readers.
2. Keep the chapters short. There's nothing more frustrating for someone who doesn't think they like to read in the first place to read for an hour or more and not even get through *one* chapter!
3. Pictures, pictures, and more pictures. Having more pictures means fewer words and less actual reading that has to be done. Someone who thinks they don't like to read is more likely to give it a try. Besides, more pictures make it look like fun!
4. What the book is about is not nearly as important as points 1, 2, and 3. Pilkey has said that even though he loved reading funny books, he would also read a sports book (as we know, he did not like sports at that age) if it had lots of pictures, large type, and short chapters.

Additionally, Pilkey makes some chapters look like comic books, while others are just one or two pages long. He also uses flip pages and silly illustrations to tell the story.

with a subject. Then a librarian in Cleveland suggested that he should write a Thanksgiving book. Voilà! As soon as he heard the idea, Pilkey knew it was what he wanted to do.

Eager to get to work and feeling inspired, he set to work. Armed with his drawing materials, a yellow writing tablet, and a quilt, he went out into the middle of a cow pasture and started writing. Then, another significant event occurred:

> All of a sudden, these cows came out of nowhere and were standing around staring at me. I was so delighted that I left my quilt and yellow notepad, and ran back across the field to grab my camera. On my way back to the cows, I noticed they were all eating something. Something yellow. As it turned out, those cows were the very first creatures on earth to get a taste of my story. They ate the whole thing up, and I had to start over from scratch. . . . At least they liked it.[2]

Everyone has heard the excuse "The dog ate my homework." But has anyone ever heard "The cows ate my manuscript"? In spite of this rough start, Pilkey eventually finished the story about a school group that takes a field trip to Mack Nugget's turkey farm and befriends the turkeys. He used Clement Clarke Moore's famous poem "A Visit from St. Nicholas," today better known by its first line "'Twas the Night Before Christmas," as his model for the text. He titled the book *'Twas the Night Before Thanksgiving.*

This book is a fine example of the kind of popular culture references that Pilkey includes in his work. The turkeys Ollie and Stanley are the author's personal salute to the film comedy team of Oliver Hardy and Stanley Laurel. Larry and Moe are named for two of The Three Stooges. Wally and Beaver take their names from the brothers on the classic television comedy *Leave It to Beaver*. And Groucho was one of the Marx Brothers.

Shown from left are the Marx Brothers—Chico, Harpo, and Groucho Marx—in a scene from* Horse Feathers *(1932), directed by Norman Z. McLeod. The classic comedy trio is another of Dav Pilkey's favorites.

Now Pilkey was ready to begin work on the illustrations. He began, logically enough, by visiting a turkey farm, where he took photos. He then painted several pictures, searching for a style that would match up with the story. (So, to answer the question of which comes first, the text or the illustrations, in Pilkey's case, it is the text.) Once he settled on a style for the art, he began work on the storyboards. These are a series of small, simple sketches that illustrators create to decide what illustrations are needed and how the drawings match up with the text.

After the storyboards were completed, he made a sample book. This handmade book is known as a "dummy," which is essentially a more detailed version of the storyboards. Most illustrators still consider these sorts of books to be fairly rough drawings. But since Pilkey did not have a publisher for his book yet, he worked hard to make them as finished and elaborate as he could.

Once the dummy was done to his satisfaction, he created the book cover. This would give publishers an idea of exactly how the finished book would look. Now, with text, illustrations, and sample cover all done, he made seven copies of the dummy, ready to be sent out to publishers to decide whether or not to publish.

To help him decide where to send his book, Pilkey bought a book called *Writer's Market*, which lists the names and addresses of publishers and describes the kinds of book each one is interested in publishing: For example, not all publishers will publish children's books. It even lists the names of some of the editors who accept manuscripts. With this information in hand, Pilkey packed up his seven precious copies, along with self-addressed stamped envelopes, and sent them off to seven different publishers. Then he anxiously awaited a response.

Unfortunately, all he received were rejection letters. He received as many as two or three rejections a week. But he was still confident. As soon as he received one of the dummy copies back from a publisher, he would pack it up again and send it to another publisher that very same day.

After several months had gone by and almost 20 publishers had rejected his manuscript, Pilkey started to feel discouraged. Maybe, he thought, *World War Won* had been a fluke. Maybe he had been wrong to think that he could be a writer. Fortunately, his friends were there to encourage him. They boosted his spirits and urged him to work on another book. Pilkey used the time to work on what would be the first of his Dragon books, all the while trying not to think too much about all those rejection letters piling up on his desk. Finally, after six months and 23 rejections, Pilkey got the letter he was waiting for: Orchard Books wanted to publish his book. *World War Won* had not been a fluke. He really was a writer and illustrator of children's books.

'Twas the Night Before Thanksgiving is now one of the most popular Thanksgiving books ever published. All of Pilkey's hard work paid off.

Reviews were excellent, with *Publishers Weekly* leading the parade of praise:

> Patterned as a parody of the celebrated Clement Moore poem, this story of eight baby turkeys unfolds with joyous abandon and crackling vitality, as eight children embark on a Thanksgiving field trip that will change their lives forever. They are breathless as they catch sight of Farmer Mack Nugget for the first time: "He was dressed all in denim,/From his head to his toe,/With a pinch of polyester/And a dash of Velcro." The exuberant turkeys—Ollie, Stanley, Larry, Moe, Wally, Beaver and Groucho—catch the children up in raucous barnyard antics until the merriment is quelled by the sight of the ax. Deeply touched by the turkeys' plight, the children—who have grown mysteriously fatter and have feathers sticking out from under their clothes—board the bus to go back to the city. The next night, family silhouettes can be seen—each with a grateful turkey guest—as "They feasted on veggies/With jelly and toast." This humorous, lighthearted story is adorned with bold, bright illustrations that convey a sense of wacky high-spiritedness sometimes lacking in traditional holiday fare.[3]

THE DRAGON BOOKS

Not content to rest on the success of *'Twas the Night Before Thanksgiving*, Pilkey worked on what would turn out to be a group of five books: the Dragon series. And while the impetus for *'Twas the Night before Thanksgiving* came from a Cleveland librarian, the Dragon series came directly from Pilkey's fertile imagination.

Dragon began his life as a happy, clumsy character that Pilkey drew on a birthday card for one of his friends. (Imagine being one of Pilkey's friends and receiving hand-drawn birthday cards from him every year!) After giving his friend the card, he forgot all about it. But months later, he saw the card sitting on a bookshelf at his friend's house. Looking at it again, Pilkey saw something in the dragon's eyes that made him think that there was something special there.

Pilkey could not stop thinking about the dragon. Several weeks later he took the card back from his friend, put it on his writing desk, and set to work. The character's simple cartoon eyes made his personality clear to Pilkey. Just like the eyes, Dragon would be a simple fellow. In fact, everything about him, from his home to his mind would be simple!

Once the outline of the character was set, the stories came quickly. He published the first three—*A Friend for Dragon*, *Dragon Gets By*, and *Dragon's Merry Christmas*—in 1991. The other two books, *Dragon's Fat Cat*, and *Dragon's Halloween*, followed soon after.

Of these, *Dragon Gets By* is a favorite of many readers for its utter silliness. Dragon spends a whole day doing everything wrong: he reads an egg, fries the morning newspaper, waters his bed, and goes to sleep on his plants. This book, which was just one silly joke after another, was the most difficult for Pilkey to write. At one point, he was so unhappy with the way it was going that he threw the manuscript away. But his editor refused to believe that the story was *that* bad. She begged him to show it to her. The editor loved the story, which made her laugh out loud. Once she changed the order of events in the story, it was ready to be published. (The book's popularity helped inspire his next series of books, but more on that later.)

Pilkey has better feelings about another book in the series, *Dragon's Merry Christmas*. Although Dragon lived alone, Pilkey still wanted to write a Christmas book about him. He realized this might be difficult since Christmas is supposed to be a happy time. Who would want to read a book about somebody spending Christmas alone? But after thinking about it, Pilkey realized that his favorite things about Christmas when he was a kid were the preparations—baking cookies, decorating the tree, and putting up lights. So that's what the book was about. "This book ended up not being the merry, joyous book that I started out to write. It ended up being kind of quiet and sweet,"[4] Pilkey said later. And that was just fine.

The first book in the Dragon series, *A Friend for Dragon*, remains one of Pilkey's favorites. Although he admits it is a very silly story, the sweetness and spirituality of the Dragon character make this particular book very special for him.

Critics loved the series. A reviewer for *Publishers Weekly* wrote of the first two titles, "With his excellent vocabulary choices and crafty characterizations . . . Pilkey has created a positively precious prehistoric prototype."[5] In *Booklist*, Carolyn Phelan raved about *Dragon's Fat Cat*: "The Dragon series is fast moving toward that pantheon of children's reading reserved for books that make kids laugh out loud . . . Again and again, Pilkey delivers."[6]

At the end of 1993, Dav Pilkey was a 25-year-old published author of five well-received children's books. It was obvious to him, his family, his friends, and to his growing number of readers that he had chosen his career wisely. Of course, there was more going on in his life than just writing and illustrating children's books. During this period, Pilkey made personal choices that sent him far from his family and childhood home.

Dav Pilkey's love of old monster movies has helped him create a number of books. For example, the Godzilla film series inspired Dogzilla, *a book with a rampaging giant canine.*

5

Changes

JUST AS DAV PILKEY was beginning to establish himself as a children's book writer, other changes were occurring in his life, which would bring him a new best friend and eventually send him on a journey to a new home, far from everyone he had ever known.

The first change occurred when Pilkey, who had lived alone since graduating college, one day found and adopted a stray puppy that quickly became his best friend. Now, you would think a creative and imaginative author like Pilkey would come up with a really interesting name for his new friend, wouldn't you? Well, not really. He named the puppy Little Dog.

Then a dream led Pilkey to make another big change. One night in 1990, he dreamed that he was destined to leave Ohio and move to Oregon, a place he had never been. For whatever reason the dream stuck with him, and in 1993, Pilkey, along with Little Dog, packed up his car and moved to Oregon. Pilkey described the trek on his Web site:

> Moving to Oregon was a great adventure for us, because Little Dog and I had never even *seen* Oregon before. We kind of felt like the early pioneers who traveled the Oregon Trail on the promise of a better life. Of course, the pioneers encountered many hardships along the way, including starvation, disease, and death.
>
> The only hardship we encountered along the way was once when we got French fries at Burger King, and they were kind of soggy.[1]

Can you imagine leaving the place where you had spent your entire life for a place you had never ever seen, just because a dream told you to?

KAT KONG AND *DOGZILLA*

Pilkey's next two books, *Kat Kong* and *Dogzilla*, were inspired by his love of old monster movies. One evening, Pilkey was at a friend's house, watching one of his favorite movies, *Godzilla vs. Megalon*. While he and his friend watched the movie, his friend's son, Nate, was sitting on the floor, peacefully building a castle using Lego blocks. The family dog, Leia, ran into the room and smashed into Nate's Lego castle. Leia towered over the fallen pieces of castle and the action figures that had inhabited it. Pilkey thought that the dog looked exactly like a figure in the

Did you know...

Dav Pilkey has been influenced by a number of famous artists, from famous painters Vincent van Gogh and Henri Rousseau to illustrators James Marshall and Marc Chagall. But there is another artist who influenced Pilkey, who created a world in which straight lines, gravity, and all the normal laws of nature did not apply. This artist's work is not found in art galleries. He was a comic strip artist whose work appeared in U.S. newspapers between 1913 and 1944.

The artist was George Herriman and the comic strip was *Krazy Kat*. Set in a dreamlike version of Herriman's vacation home of Coconino County, Arizona, the strip focuses on a curious "love triangle." The strip's title character, Krazy Kat, is a carefree and innocent cat whose gender is in question (he/she is referred to as both male and female throughout the strip). Ignatz Mouse is the cat's enemy. A protective police dog, Officer Bull Pupp, completes the triangle. Krazy Kat is in love with Ignatz. But Ignatz hates Krazy and loves to throw bricks at Krazy's head. Krazy takes this as a sign of Ignatz's affection. Officer Pupp, who loves Krazy, makes it his mission to interfere with Ignatz's brick-throwing schemes and lock the mouse in jail.

The basic plot, as you can see, is simple. But Herman's visual and verbal creativity, which created a dreamlike, ever-changing world for his characters, made *Krazy Kat* one of the very first comics to be seen as a work of art. And Hermann's work continues to influence the creators of many comic books and animated films.

Pilkey has saluted Herriman and *Krazy Kat* in his books. In *Kat Kong*, the three mice explorers sail on a ship called the USS *Ignatz*, named, of course, for Harriman's brick-throwing mouse!

movie, standing triumphant over a destroyed city. This might also make a terrific book, he thought.

This idea became two books: *Kat Kong*, with a monster cat, and *Dogzilla*, with a rampaging canine hero. The artwork for these two books is a witty combination of photographs of dogs, cats, and mice on colorfully imaginative hand-painted backgrounds. The combination of photographs and artwork was a new style for Pilkey. He was sure that it would appeal to his growing band of readers.

These books proved difficult to illustrate and came close to never being published! After working on the project for six months, Pilkey sent the stories, the dummies, and sample artwork for both books to his publisher. He expected to receive a quick acceptance. Imagine his surprise and dismay when, months later (on Christmas Eve), he opened his mailbox to find a letter from his publishers telling him that they were not interested in either book! (On his Web site, Pilkey notes that that Christmas was his worst ever, even worse than the one in 1969 when he threw up while sitting on Santa's lap at a local department store.)

Heartbroken, Pilkey almost gave up on ever having the two books published. But six months later, another editor was visiting him at his studio. When she saw the painting of *Dogzilla* on the wall, she loved it, and expressed the wish that she could publish a book like that. It turned out to be her lucky day; he had two books like that nearly ready to go, and she immediately agreed to publish both of them.

It took Pilkey many long months of hard work to complete the artwork. Photographing animals is never easy, and getting them to make the expressions that Pilkey needed for his book took every trick he knew. To get

King Kong, *directed by Merian C. Cooper and Ernest B. Schoedsack, is considered by many critics and fans to be one of the best monster movies of all time. Since its release in 1933, it has inspired numerous imitators. Dav Pilkey's book* Kat Kong *was written in homage to this film masterpiece.*

his cat Blueberry to say "meow," Pilkey had to blow on her head. And Leia would only lift her ears if he asked if she wanted to go for a walk. He even had to build a little platform around a vase filled with water so that the mice would stay still long enough to be photographed. Sometimes it was impossible to get the animals exactly in the pose he needed. In some of the final artwork, Pilkey combined a head from one photograph with the arms and legs from another.

When *Dogzilla* and *Kat Kong* were published in 1993, both received excellent reviews from readers and reviewers alike. A critic for *Publishers Weekly* noted:

> In a bold departure for Pilkey . . . these two brazenly funny picture books spoof Godzilla and King Kong as they launch the mice inhabitants of Mousopolis against, respectively, a killer cat and dog. Touched-up photos of the author's pets are set against fluorescent cityscapes and luminous skylines. The texts ripple with corny but kid-pleasing puns ("The Big Cheese tried to catch up to the hog dog with all the relish he could muster") and shameless gags ("'What are you, men or mice?' 'Mice,' they squeaked.'"), while the pictures are packed with sly allusions . . . Pilkey's exuberance is irresistible.[2]

HOW DUMB CAN THEY BE?

Dav Pilkey's next series would bring him even greater fame as a master of silliness. The Dumb Bunnies series was inspired by an unlikely source, Pilkey's least favorite of his own books, *Dragon Gets By*. He often found himself wondering why the book was so popular with readers. There was no story. It was just a series of jokes and puns. Then it hit him that that was exactly why the books were so popular. After all, one of his favorite series of children's books was *The Stupids* by Harry Allard and James Marshall. The characters in those books are unable to understand the simplest concepts and tasks.

Pilkey had longed to create a series of books similar to *The Stupids*, but could not figure out how to go about it, or even how to choose the characters. But, as he said later,

> ... late one night it just hit me. I was walking my dog in the rain along the Willamette River in Eugene, Oregon. We stopped to look at the river, then suddenly I thought: "The Dumb Bunnies!" I started thinking about all the funny things I could do with these silly characters and began to smile. Before long I was giggling. I think I spent about an hour out there in the cold, pouring rain, just looking at the river and laughing my head off.[3]

The four books in the series, published between 1994 and 1997, use brightly colored illustrations and straight-faced narratives to describe the adventures of a family of clueless bunnies. Within the stories, Pilkey made fun of other stories. In the first book, *Dumb Bunnies*, famous fables such as "The Three Little Bears" and "Little Red Riding Hood" are used. Little Red Goldilocks wreaks havoc in the Bunnies' home—until Baby Bunny flushes her down the toilet!

In *The Dumb Bunnies' Easter*, holiday customs are completely confused. The Bunny family goes to the beach during a storm in *Make Way for Dumb Bunnies*. And near havoc ensues when they release the animals from their cages in *The Dumb Bunnies Go to the Zoo*. In *The Bulletin of the Center for Children's Books*, Roger Sutton noted the relationship between the Dumb Bunnies and the Stupids, calling them "The Stupids in pink fur."[4] In *Booklist*, Mary Harris Veeder praised *The Dumb Bunnies' Easter*: "The Bunny family is a worthy successor to those all-time favorites the Stupids ... This is dumbness supreme and a real treat."[5]

The Dumb Bunnies series is among Pilkey's most popular works. An animated television series ran on CBS from 1998 to 1999. But when the books were originally published, they did not name Dav Pilkey as the author! Instead, they were published under the name Sue Denim. Sue was a rather shy author. Pilkey described her as a "rising star among authors who write dumb stories."[6] So who is Sue Denim?

On his Web site, Pilkey explains that he had always wanted to write a book using a pseudonym—a fake name that authors sometimes use in order to hide their real identities. (For example, the American author Joyce Carol Oates, noted for her literary novels, published a series of mystery novels under the pseudonym Rosamond Smith.) Pilkey picked the name Sue Denim as his pseudonym because when you say it out loud it sounds *exactly* like the word *pseudonym*!

Pilkey even created an entirely fictional background for Denim. Her "biography" included a list of fake book titles she had supposedly written: *The Wonderful World of American Cheese*, *Tippy the Ninja's Irritating Skin Rash, Billy the Tap-Dancing Dental Hygienist*, and *Fun with Harsh Chemicals and Detergents*. Pilkey even posed for publicity photos as Sue. He wore a black wig and glasses purchased at a joke shop and borrowed lipstick and makeup.

You can imagine his shock then, when after the publication of the Dumb Bunnies books, fan mail started pouring in for his made-up author. There were even times when Sue Denim received more fan letters than Pilkey! Imagine coming in second to your own made-up character! Of course, Pilkey was able to laugh at the ridiculousness of the situation.

The popularity of the Dumb Bunnies series solidified Pilkey's position as America's foremost writer and illustrator of silliness for children. And Pilkey being Pilkey, there was more silliness to come. But Dav Pilkey has a serious side as well. His first book to show that side of him brought his greatest critical acclaim to date and an award he never imagined he would win.

Pictured, Vincent van Gogh's 1889 painting The Starry Night. *An illustration in Dav Pilkey's award-winning book* The Paperboy *was inspired by this famous work.*

6

Breakthrough

BY 1995, PILKEY had published 16 children's books, all of varying degrees of fun and silliness. His next book, *The Paperboy*, would be his first "serious" children's book. It was inspired, in part, by his own childhood.

Like many 13-year-old boys, Pilkey had delivered newspapers to earn extra money. In his case the paper was the *Lorain Journal*. He hated getting up early in the morning to deliver the papers. What he did enjoy, though, was the calm and independence he felt while riding his bike through the quiet early morning streets of Elyria, Ohio. But never in his wildest imagination did young David ever think that he would write a book about the experience when he grew up.

In fact, he never gave the subject a second thought until one morning while he was walking Little Dog and saw his own paperboy riding his bicycle, delivering papers just as he had done so many years ago. Seeing his paperboy in the early mornings stirred in him the memories of how he had felt when he had been a paperboy. He decided to write a story based on his memories about his first job.

As is often the case with writing, this was easier said than done. Pilkey knew he wanted to write a story about being a paperboy, but then he got stuck. He was unable to come up with a good story. So he put the idea aside for a while and worked on other books. Then the idea for the book came back to life in a most surprising way.

Pilkey woke up one day with the story completely laid out in his head. He quickly grabbed a pencil and notebook. (Like many writers, Pilkey keeps the tools of his trade nearby at all times, including next to the bed. You never know when inspiration might strike!) Within 15 minutes he had written out the entire text. He completed the illustrations for the book, which were acrylic paintings, almost as quickly. As Pilkey recalled, "I had to hurry up and finish it so I could start painting *Make Way for Dumb Bunnies*."[1]

The Paperboy received some of the best reviews of Pilkey's career. *Publishers Weekly* led the cheers:

> Pilkey is at his best in this highly atmospheric work. Here his trademark color palette glows quietly under the cover of darkness; violet skies and emerald-shadowed fields predominate until the explosion of a fiery dawn. Early one cold morning a boy and his dog rise to deliver newspapers. In almost reverential silence they eat breakfast, prepare the newspapers, then step out into the chill, leaving sleeping parents and sister inside. Pilkey perfectly captures the thrill of being out early,

> seeing the world so new and having it all to oneself. Something magical is at work on this most ordinary of paper routes, tangible in the controlled hush of the narrative and in the still, moon-lit landscapes. And, at last, as his family awakens to golden sunlight, the paperboy returns to his bed, prepared to enter another familiar world: dreamland.[2]

Other critics agreed. Wendy Lukehart, writing for the *School Library Journal*, raved that Pilkey "paints their [the paperboy and his dog's] experience with a graceful economy of language . . . [it] is a totally satisfying story."[3] Carolyn Phelan, writing in *Booklist*, made special note of the book's illustrations, which "include beautifully composed landscapes and interiors, ending with a Chagall-like dream scene on the last page. An evocative mood piece, this captures the elusive feeling of being outside before dawn."[4]

The reference to painter Marc Chagall must have been particularly gratifying to Pilkey, who had long considered the artist as one of his favorites. (Pilkey referenced another of his favorite painters in *The Paperboy*. One of the illustrations was inspired by one of van Gogh's most famous paintings, *The Starry Night*.) Still, as gratifying as the reviews were, it seems unlikely that they could have compared to the moment when Pilkey learned that *The Paperboy* had been selected for a major award.

The Caldecott Medal is presented annually to the "artist of the most distinguished American Picture Book for Children published in the United States during the preceding year."[5] One book wins the Caldecott Medal and three or four others are named Caldecott Honor books. *The Paperboy* was named an Honor Book in 1997. For Pilkey, who was still best known for books about dumb bunnies, rampaging dogs and cats destroying mouse cities, and gentle dragons, being recognized in this way was an incredible honor. He was completely surprised and very grateful to receive the award.

Did you know...

Dav Pilkey's books have sold millions of copies. Yet he has not received many awards. Why is that?

One reason is that many parents, teachers, and critics find Pilkey's books, loaded with potty humor, extraordinarily dumb bunnies, naughty cafeteria ladies from outer space, wedgies, and uranium unicorns from Uranus, too silly. They are not serious enough to be worthy of an award. But there is more to it than that. Throughout the arts, the art of being funny is taken less seriously than the art of being serious.

For example, a comedy has not won the Academy Award for Best Picture since Woody Allen's *Annie Hall* won in 1977. Actors have a much better chance of winning an Oscar for playing a dramatic role than a comedic one. In literature, serious novels are the ones that win the Pulitzer Prize, the Caldecott Medal, and the Nobel Prize. Being funny might make millions laugh, but it generally does not lead to awards.

But while drama wins awards, seriousness does not necessarily translate into popularity or longevity. It is entirely possible that generations of young readers will still be enjoying the adventures of Captain Underpants long after *The Paperboy* and other Caldecott winners are forgotten.

A NEW AUDIENCE

Following his now fairly established pattern, his next books were yet another new series. And while they, too, were humorous, they aimed at an audience Pilkey had never written for before, one even younger than his usual readers.

The Big Dog and Little Dog series was written for babies and toddlers. The books were printed on thick cardboard so they were difficult to rip or tear and used minimal text and extra large, colorful illustrations. Big Dog is based on Martha Jane, a dog that belonged to friends of Pilkey's. Little Dog is based on Pilkey's pet of the same name.

The stories are basic and uncomplicated: the two doggie friends go on walks, splash in puddles, snuggle together, get in trouble after being left alone in the house, and even wear sweaters! In the sixth and last book in the series, *Big Dog and Little Dog Making a Mistake*, the two canine friends confuse a skunk for a kitten. Then they create havoc at a party. The text for this book took Pilkey only five minutes to write. The illustrations took him almost two and a half weeks!

Critics responded to the heartwarming adventures of Big Dog and Little Dog. Writing in *School Library Journal*, Maura Bresnahan predicted that babies and toddlers would find "the colorful illustrations appealing, but the humor will be better appreciated by older children."[6] She also noted that the simple sentence structure and repetitive text "makes this board book ideal for those just learning to read."[7]

CAPTAIN UNDERPANTS RETURNS

Although Pilkey has disliked doing interviews ever since his first book was published in 1987, he has always enjoyed visiting schools and libraries and speaking to kids. (Unfortunately, stomach problems have now made it nearly impossible for Pilkey to travel, so he does very few speaking engagements.) He never gives just a boring talk. He prepares a presentation in which he draws pictures and tells the story of how he became an author and illustrator. But of all the stories Pilkey would tell during these presentations, the most popular were the ones about his second grade creation, Captain Underpants.

Pilkey would stand at the board and draw a picture of a slightly chubby superhero while telling the kids about creating his own comic books. Then he would tell his audience the name of the character he was drawing. Naturally, the moment he said the magic words "Captain Underpants" the entire crowd would burst out laughing. After all, just hearing a grown-up say the word "underpants" can be pretty funny! Pilkey recalled to *Publishers Weekly*:

> Inevitably, the name "Captain Underpants" would come up, and though I cracked jokes throughout my presentation, the mention of this name would get by far the biggest laugh. And whenever I mentioned the title of one of my early Captain Underpants comic books, which involved talking toilets, the room would explode with laughter.[8]

After finishing his presentation, Pilkey would ask the audience if they had any questions. Invariably, one of the first questions was "Are you ever going to write a book about Captain Underpants?" The fact is that from the moment he began writing children's books, Pilkey had planned to write about his childhood creation. He had come up with several different versions of the story, including a 48-page comic book. But every publisher who saw the stories about Captain Underpants turned them down.

This changed in the mid-1990s. Because of his string of popular books, publishers were eager to publish whatever

Pilkey wanted to write. So he felt the time was right to create a series of Captain Underpants books. He had the skills necessary to successfully combine a story with illustrations. And he knew what made kids laugh. In 1997, the world received the first installment in what would become Pilkey's most successful book series.

The first book in the series, *The Adventures of Captain Underpants: An Epic Novel*, sets the stage for the books that followed. The main characters are introverted Harold Hutchins and extroverted George Beard, two mischievous fourth graders who write their own comic books. Pilkey readily admits that Harold and George represent the opposite sides of the author's personality. The book's heroes are allied against their mutual enemy: the cranky principal, Mr. Krupp. The boys hypnotize Mr. Krupp with a 3-D Hypno-Ring. From then on, the once-crabby principal is transformed into Captain Underpants whenever he hears fingers snapped. Wearing only tight white underwear and a cape and carrying a roll of toilet paper, Captain Underpants fights for "Truth, Justice, and ALL that is Pre-shrunk and Cottony."

Pilkey's underwear-clad crime fighter tackles criminals such as bank robbers by giving them wedgies. He also confronts a mad scientist, the evil Dr. Diaper, who like every mad scientist, has plans to control the world. By distracting the doctor with doggy-doo, Harold, George, and Captain Underpants save the day. The boys then dehypnotize their principal and get him back into his street clothes before he knows what happened.

You might be wondering where Pilkey got the idea for the all-important Hypno-Ring in Captain Underpants. He claims it was inspired by the ads he saw in comic books and magazines as a kid. Pilkey and his friends would always

The Our Gang *film shorts, also known as* The Little Rascals, *were a television staple for decades and were among Dav Pilkey's favorites. Shown from left are some of the most famous Rascals: Bobby "Wheezer" Hutchins, Norman "Chubby" Chaney, Jackie Cooper, Allen "Farina" Hoskins, Matthew "Stymie" Beard, three unidentified boys, Mary Ann Jackson, Dorothy DeBorba, Shirley Jean Rickert, and Pete the Pup.*

send away for such items as "monster ghosts" and "x-ray glasses," but of course, none of the items actually worked. While writing Captain Underpants, he thought it would be funny if George and Harold sent away for one of the same kind of items that he used to order himself, but in their case the item actually worked!

You might also ask where Pilkey come up with the names of George Beard and Harold Hutchins in the first place. The main characters' first names come from characters in two of Pilkey's favorite books: George was taken from *Georgie the Ghost* and Harold from *Harold and the Purple Crayon*. And their last names? Beard and Hutchins were the last names of two of Pilkey's favorite characters from the Little Rascals films: Stimey (played by Matthew Beard) and Wheezer (played by Bobby Hutchins).

Pilkey's imaginative story is illustrated with equally creative black-and-white cartoons; and he even "animates" a chapter by using what he calls "Flip-o-Rama," a device that allows readers to flip the pages back and forth to create an animated effect instead of describing the action himself with words. This trick goes back to his childhood, as he told an interviewer for *Nickelodeon Magazine*:

> When I was a kid, my friend and I used to make "Flip-O-Ramas" all the time in school (but back then we called them "Flip-Actions"). We thought these pictures were funny, but they used to really irritate our teachers. My dream is that kids everywhere will learn to make their own "Flip-O-Rama," and use them to annoy humorless grown-ups throughout the world![9]

With its combination of grossly funny text and comic book-like illustrations, the book was a smash hit with young readers. But parents, teachers, and other grown-ups, such as critics, had mixed feelings about the whole thing. (To this day, the book remains one of Pilkey's own personal favorites, and is the one he has read the most—at least 15 times!)

Writing in *Booklist*, Stephanie Zvirin complained that the silliness "goes overboard . . . and the many action-packed illustrations rob the plot of some of its zip by commanding more than their share of attention," while acknowledging that Pilkey's "humor is on target for some kids in this age group."[10] History seemed to be repeating itself: the grown-ups still found his sense of humor to be a little too gross and juvenile, just as they did when he was a kid.

Indeed, while *The Adventures of Captain Underpants: An Epic Novel* brought Dav Pilkey's popularity with his young readers to even greater heights, a backlash soon began to develop among adults who felt that it was inappropriate for young readers. The arguments both for and against Captain Underpants—and Dav Pilkey's work in general—would increase in number with each new book in the series.

Dav Pilkey's Captain Underpants has battled talking toilets and Professor Poopypants, but is often met with criticism by educators, including one high school principal who banned students from dressing up as the children's book character. Despite this, the series remains wildly popular with young readers.

7

New Challenges

ON HIS WEB SITE, Dav Pilkey explains his goal in writing *The Adventures of Captain Underpants*. He wanted to write a book stylistically identical to that of a picture book, but to do it in a way that was more suitable for young readers, with very short chapters in which the illustrations were just as important (and as plentiful) as the words. By doing this, he hoped to create a book that even kids who would never voluntarily pick up a book would want to read.

It worked, probably beyond his wildest dreams. The first Captain Underpants book was very successful when it was first published in 1997. Two years later, in 1999, he published the second book in the series, *Captain Underpants and the Attack of the Talking Toilets*. The plot for this one was taken directly from the comic book he had written about the character when he was in third grade. The story involves school brain Melvin's science project—a copying machine that changes images into matter. George and Harold use the invention to reproduce their latest comic book. In doing so, the pair releases an army of teacher-eating toilets led by the evil Turbo Toilet 2000. Captain Underpants saves the day with the aid of Wedgie Power and his Incredible Robo-Plunger. And George and Harold were made school principals for a day.

Later that year, *Captain Underpants and the Invasion of the Incredibly Naughty Cafeteria Ladies from Outer Space* was published. In this story, our intrepid heroes George and Harold fool the cafeteria staff into baking cupcakes that flood Jerome Horwitz Elementary School with sticky green goo. After the cafeteria ladies quit, Principal Krupp inadvertently hires three space aliens named Zorx, Klax, and Jennifer to take their places. When the aliens begin turning students into zombie nerds, Harold, George, and Captain Underpants are once again called into action. In the end, they save the world from an alien invasion. Reviewing *Captain Underpants and the Attack of the Talking Toilets*, a *Booklist* critic predicted it was "destined to be as popular as the first book," while a reviewer in *Horn Book* called it "part graphic novel, part tongue-in-cheek parody, . . . very hip and funny."[1]

In *Captain Underpants and the Perilous Plot of Professor Poopypants*, the boys manage to enrage Professor Pippy P. Poopypants, a scientific genius who gets no respect because of his name—imagine that! When the inevitable chaos ensues, it once again falls on Captain Underpants to save the day. In *Captain Underpants and the Wrath of the Wicked Wedgie Woman*, the retirement of hated teacher Miss Ribble leads to the creation of the evil Wedgie Woman, who is armed with horrible robots and an even more horrible hairstyle. Her mission to conquer the world is halted, of course, by Captain Underpants.

Books six and seven in the series are Parts 1 and 2 of *Captain Underpants and the Big, Bad Battle of the Bionic Booger Boy*. In Part 1, *The Night of the Nasty Nostril Nuggets*, school brain Melvin accidentally transforms himself into the giant Bionic Booger Boy, who produces (naturally) robo-boogers. Although the threat of robo-boogers seems to be eliminated in Part 2, *The Revenge of the Ridiculous Robo-Boogers*, it returns stronger than ever in the middle of a power shift that renders Captain Underpants powerless while a school toilet is transformed into a time machine. Despite the complicated plot, JoAnn Jonas, writing in *School Library Journal*, called the two-part epic "witty, fun, and full of adventure."[2]

And indeed, while many critics, such as Tim Wadham in *School Library Journal*, called Captain Underpants "one of

Did you know...

Dav Pilkey never ate cafeteria food until he started visiting schools as an adult author. It seems that the small parochial schools that he went to when he was growing up did not offer school lunch programs. Instead, Pilkey and his classmates would have to bring their own lunches from home; he was particularly proud of his very cool *Planet of the Apes* lunchbox.

the best series to get reluctant readers reading,"[3] and in the same magazine Marlene Gawron observed that the "fun" of the Underpants books "is in the reading, which is full of puns, rhymes, and nonsense along with enough revenge and wish fulfillment for every downtrodden fun-seeking kid who never wanted to read a book,"[4] others, felt differently. Much like the teachers and adults of Pilkey's youth, they were offended by the books' humor and disrespectful attitude. Not content, though, to just criticize the books, some felt so strongly about the books that they attempted to have them banned from school libraries.

THE CRITICS FIRE BACK

A CNN report on the furor over Captain Underpants noted that many of Pilkey's critics are parents who dislike the use of what they see as "potty humor" in the books. "Bathroom talk is something you're trying to teach them *not* to do, and these books are encouraging them to do it," said one parent.[5] Many teachers also too often fail to appreciate Pilkey's tales of pranks gone out of control and his characters' sassy backtalk and disregard for authority. "Students want to mime that behavior, instead of being on task," said a first grade teacher in Texas. "It's very counterproductive for a teacher."[6] Yet Sam Butterfield, a young Captain Underpants fan in Massachusetts, pointed out that "grown-ups . . . say the books are vulgar. But it's just funny writing, you know?"[7] Unsurprisingly, Pilkey refuses to take his critics too seriously, as you can see in the transcript of an interview he did with CNN:

CNN: What do you say to parents—and I understand some have complained—who claim your books encourage crude, bathroom humor?

PILKEY: I don't say anything to them. I just stick out my tongue and make rude noises.

CNN: What about another parental complaint: That your books encourage kids to be disrespectful—that Captain Underpants turns kids into smarty pants?

Did you know...

Librarians, administrators, teachers, and parents have threatened to remove the Captain Underpants series and *The Adventures of Super Diaper Baby* from school and public libraries. But Pilkey is not the only author to have faced the threat of being banned.

The American Library Association (ALA) has reported that across the United States more than one book a day faces being removed from open access in schools and libraries. In 2006, for example, there were 546 known attempts to remove books from school and library shelves. Shockingly, in some parts of the country, books are still burned in an attempt to stop others from reading them. In late 2001, for example, several hundred members of a church in Alamogordo, New Mexico, burned a pile of Harry Potter books. They claimed that the books promoted witchcraft and the powers of darkness.

According to the American Library Association's Library Bill of Rights, only parents have the right to restrict their children's access to certain books. No one else, the ALA feels, has the right to restrict a child's access to library materials.

Fortunately, there are ways for young readers to fight back against censorship. Thanks to the organization kidSPEAK, kids now have a voice, for, as kidSPEAK states, "Kids have First Amendment rights—and kidSPEAK helps kids fight for them!"

PILKEY: For that one, I usually just cup my left hand into my right armpit and pump my right arm up and down, creating a lovely flatulence noise.

CNN: And the final, perhaps most serious criticism: That the books give kids ideas for "acting out"—disrupting class, vandalizing school property?

PILKEY: Do you notice a trend here? Grown-ups do a lot of complaining! To be serious for a moment, I almost never hear complaints like that. I get thousands of letters each year from teachers and librarians who use these books in their schools, and with the exception of two or three letters, they've all been very positive. The thing I hear over and over again, is how grateful educators are that these books have turned their kids on to reading.[8]

Unfortunately, some critics of his books have gone beyond writing letters to Pilkey to complain about his books. Some have tried to remove the books from school library shelves. In an elementary school in Naugatuck, Connecticut, the books were banned after school officials claimed that they were inspiring bad behavior in fourth graders. The *Dallas Morning News* reported that the principal's explanation for banning the books was simple: "The boys started getting whooped up at Captain Underpants, saying things like 'You're in your underpants.'"[9] Pilkey and other banned authors find it hard to believe that someone would try to stop kids from reading books they actually enjoy reading. But it does happen.

Indeed, on the American Library Association's list of the 10 most challenged books between the years 2000 and 2005, Dav Pilkey's Captain Underpants series clocks in at number nine! Some of the other books on the list are J.K. Rowling's Harry Potter series, John Steinbeck's classic novel *Of Mice and Men*, Maya Angelou's memoir *I Know Why the Caged Bird Sings*, and Judy Blume's *Forever*.

Still, as the creator of Captain Underpants, Pilkey has mixed feelings when he learns that his books have been banned. On the one hand, he loves when such book bannings are reported since the publicity usually guarantees even more people will want to read his works. On the other hand, he feels bad when people attack his books and his characters. After all, in some ways, they are attacking him personally!

Despite the controversy surrounding Pilkey's work, the popularity of his books remains undiminished. The books have been translated into a number of languages, including Portuguese, Danish, French, German, Greek, Norwegian, Polish, Russian, Japanese, and Hebrew. Obviously, there's something universal in the appeal of Pilkey's sense of humor, and jokes about toilets, wedgies, and poopypants transcend national boundaries. As a reviewer pointed out in *Publishers Weekly*, "Those with a limited tolerance for the silly need not apply to the Captain Underpants fan club, yet its legion members will plunge happily into his latest bumbling adventure."[10]

The popularity of Captain Underpants led Pilkey to create a spin-off, *The Adventures of Super Diaper Baby: The First Graphic Novel.* The authors of this book were listed as George Beard and Harold Hutchins. Presenting the book as being written by George and Harold was an interesting challenge for Pilkey. The boys are given a writing assignment and are told that Captain Underpants cannot appear in their story. So George and Harold tell a tale about a baby that is sprayed with super power juice shortly after birth. Super Diaper Baby begins his crime-fighting career by wadding up a villain in toilet paper.

Critics responded warmly to the book. *Publishers Weekly* called it "preposterously good-humored"[11] and Piper L. Nyman describing it as "another goofy, gross-out selection from a popular author."[12] A critic for *Kirkus Reviews* noted:

"Adults will want to use this book as birdcage liner, and young readers with elementary senses of humor will revel in the . . . silliness."[13] That reviewer's words proved to be accurate. In the summer of 2003, the Riverside Unified School District in Riverside, California, considered banning the book. A student's grandmother had filed a formal complaint asking the district to remove it from the district's libraries and classrooms.

The *Los Angeles Times* described the book as "125 pages of potty humor, purposely misspelled words, and—critics say—overall disregard for authority."[14] Pilkey's sense of humor had once again rubbed some parents and teachers the wrong way. But Sue Tavaligone, a parent and committee member, summed up the feelings of a number of board members: "I don't like the idea of poop being in the story, but it is pretty creative."[15] Betty Schmechel, a specialist in English and language arts, said, "At first blush, I don't want to see this book become a model for students. But I also support the freedom to read. That's the dilemma."[16] Pilkey weighed in on the controversy on his Web site: "It was never my intention to offend anybody. My intention with this book was to make kids laugh. If a kid is reading my books and laughing, I've done my job."[17]

Pilkey also pointed out that the book's misspelled words and bad grammar mattered little, because the comics that George and Harold had created were good as well as funny. His hope was that kids would notice the mistakes but move beyond them. He wanted to help them realize that sometimes perfect spelling and grammar and artwork matter less than trying to be creative without the fear of making a mistake.

Ultimately, the Riverside board voted to allow the book to remain in the libraries and classrooms. Fortunately,

Pilkey was able to beat the forces of censorship. But it had been a close call for those who believe that kids should be allowed to read whatever they want to read.

Captain Underpants had made Pilkey popular and beloved beyond his wildest dreams. But he did not want to write only Captain Underpants books for the rest of his life. He had a lot of new ideas. There were also changes coming in his personal life that would add to his already happy existence.

Shown from left are William Frawley, Vivian Vance, Lucille Ball, and Desi Arnaz, the stars of the 1950s television sitcom I Love Lucy. *The name of Arnaz's character, Ricky Ricardo, was the inspiration for Dav Pilkey's Ricky Ricotta series.*

8

Having It All

IN 1999, SHORTLY AFTER the publication of the first two Captain Underpants books, Pilkey (along with Little Dog) decided it was time to leave Oregon. They moved north to the state of Washington and settled on a small island. There, they enjoyed the island's natural beauty and often took long walks on the beach. They even kayaked together! (Little Dog also enjoys sitting in Pilkey's lap while he works.)

One of the pair's favorite pastimes was to walk to the island's only sushi restaurant. Pilkey is a strict vegetarian and does not eat seafood, so the restaurant's owner, Sayuri (pronounced Sy-you-dee), made vegetarian sushi rolls just for him. She also allowed Little Dog in the restaurant. He would happily sit under the table eating the chicken dinner that Sayuri had prepared especially for him. Soon, Dav and Sayuri fell in love. They were married in 2005 on the beach under a full moon.

ENTERING THE WORLD OF SCIENCE FICTION

Between 2000 and 2005, five more Captain Underpants books were published. But Pilkey had also been working on another series. The main character was Ricky Ricotta, a mouse who befriends a giant robot.

One of Pilkey's favorite childhood TV shows was called *Super Host*. The show featured a red-nosed guy dressed in an ill-fitting Superman costume who performed skits and showed old monster movies. Pilkey's favorite movies were the old Japanese monster movies. "I loved seeing the giant monsters crashing through cities, with all the little people below running and screaming. It always looked kinda fake, but I still loved it."[1] Once again, Pilkey would prove that activities like watching old monster movies are *not* a complete waste of time.

Pilkey set to work on the new series. He completed the text for the first book, *Ricky Ricotta's Mighty Robot*. He drew sketches of the main characters and sent everything to his publisher, Scholastic, where it sat for a couple of years.

Why the delay? Pilkey wanted to illustrate the Ricky Ricotta books himself, but deep down he knew that he was not the right artist for the series. "The books needed bold, strong linework, and a comic book sense of action and perspective. That style of illustrating just doesn't come naturally for me."[2] So, for the first time, Pilkey was writing a series that he would not illustrate himself. But how would he find the right illustrator for the job? Eventually, fate and a love of books did the trick.

One day, Pilkey walked into a small bookstore in Portland, Oregon. He was amazed by what he saw. Hanging on the store's walls were some of the "coolest paintings that Dav had ever seen."[3] The artist was named Martin Ontiveros, and his artwork featured just the things that Pilkey was looking for: giant robots, monsters, and space monkeys. He had found his illustrator.

Ontiveros had never illustrated a children's book, but Pilkey convinced him to give it a try. Pilkey had already done rough sketches of the book's main characters, Ricky, his parents, and the mighty robot. He turned them over to Ontiveros, who redrew the characters in bold, broad lines, completely making them his own. After Ontiveros designed and drew sketches of the book's supporting characters, including Dr. Stinky McNasty, Pilkey showed the new artwork to his editor at Scholastic. The editor agreed that Ontiveros should illustrate the entire series.

The first book, *Ricky Ricotta's Mighty Robot*, lays the groundwork for the series. A lonely little mouse, Ricky Ricotta, makes friends with a giant robot that takes on the school bullies and rescues the city of Squeakyville from an evil rat scientist, the infamous Dr. Stinky McNasty. The other book titles make clear what each one is about: *Ricky Ricotta's Mighty Robot vs. the Mutant Mosquitoes from Mercury*; *Ricky Ricotta's Mighty Robot vs. the Voodoo Vultures from Venus*; *Ricky Ricotta's Mighty Robot vs. the Mecha Monkeys from Mars*; *Ricky Ricotta's Mighty Robot vs. the Jurassic Jackrabbits from Jupiter*; and the classic *Ricky Ricotta's Mighty Robot vs. the Stupid Stinkbugs from Saturn*. (Note how Pilkey uses alliteration—repeating the same letter at the start of each word—to

Did you know...

Dav Pilkey is clearly a big fan of television. As a boy, he treasured the time he was allowed to watch television. Because children typically did not have televisions in their rooms in those days, it was easy for his parents to use a threat of "no television tonight" to get him to behave, at least reasonably well.

Unlike most writers, Pilkey has no objection to kids watching television. He has made the point that for as long as he can remember, adults have blamed TV for destroying young minds and filling them with senseless violence and useless cartoons. But, Pilkey notes, before television, adults were blaming *radio* for all that was wrong with young people. And before that, adults blamed *books* for ruining society, leading to all kinds of ills, including depression, bad eyesight, and even madness!

One of Pilkey's favorite shows when he was young was *I Love Lucy*. It starred Lucille Ball as a housewife trying to get into show business. Her real-life husband, Desi Arnaz, played a Cuban bandleader. In *Ricky Ricotta's Mighty Robot vs. the Jurassic Jackrabbits from Jupiter*, Ricky's cousin makes her first appearance. Her name? Lucy! *Ricky Ricotta's Mighty Robot vs. the Stupid Stinkbugs from Saturn* features Lucy's mother and father. Their names? Aunt Ethyl and Uncle Freddy—the names of the neighbors on *I Love Lucy*, Fred and Ethel Mertz. And Lucille Ball played a character named Lucy Ricardo. Her husband's name on the show was Ricky Ricardo! Sound like any other character you know?

make even the *titles* of his books funny: *Stupid Stinkbugs from Saturn*.)

Of course, even the silliest books have a smidgen of seriousness about them. Pilkey has always been fond of poking fun at classic works of art and literature. But, did you know that the second book in the Ricky Ricotta series, *The Mutant Mosquitoes from Mercury*, is based on William Shakespeare's classic historical play *Henry IV, Part I*? (Actually, this is not true at all. But Pilkey devoted two entire pages on his Web site to describing how he and illustrator Ontiveros carefully turned Shakespeare's epic play into a children's book about a mouse and a Mighty Robot—a perfect example of Pilkey's mischievous sense of fun!)

STILL THE CLASS CLOWN

Today, Pilkey is happily married and the author or illustrator of more than 40 books. He has won critical success, financial freedom, and the adoration of legions of young readers around the world—not bad for a kid who could not concentrate in school, a kid who spent more time sitting in the hallway than in the classroom, a kid whose only distinction in school was his ability to make his classmates laugh.

Staying in touch with his childhood has enabled Pilkey to become such a successful writer of humorous children's books. There is still a part of him that has never grown up. Part of him is still a second grader who knows exactly what it takes to get kids to pick up a book, especially kids who don't really *like* to read! Pilkey's ability to speak to kids without seeming forced or unnatural is what makes kids love his books. Reading one of Pilkey's books is like having the funniest, most talented kid in your class tell you stories and make you laugh till it hurts. Pilkey has held on to the freedom to create without embarrassment and he finds inspiration for his art from children. He notes:

> Children often send me pictures they've drawn, and I'm always amazed at the way they present shape and color. Children are natural impressionists. They're not afraid to make their trees purple and yellow, and it's okay if the sky is green with red stripes. . . . When children are drawing, anything goes! Of course, you know that one day an art teacher is going to grab hold of these kids and turn them all into accountants, but while they are still fresh and naïve, children can create some of the freshest and most beautiful art there is.[4]

By holding on to his inner child, Pilkey has crafted some of the freshest children's books written in America. By never changing who he is, by channeling his love of art and silliness into his work, by defying the people who said he would never amount to anything, he was able to grow up and do what he always wanted to do. He writes on his Web site:

> When I was a kid making silly books out in the hall, I never dreamed that one day I'd be making silly books for a living. The coolest thing is that I used to get in trouble for being the class clown . . . and now it's my job.[5]

Getting paid to be the class clown—nice work if you can get it. As long as Dav Pilkey enjoys "making silly books," young readers will continue to read them. And we all look forward to seeing what America's class clown will come up with next.

CHRONOLOGY

1966 David Pilkey is born on March 4 to David M. and Barbara Pilkey in Cleveland, Ohio.

1983 When a malfunctioning label maker at Pizza Hut prints out Pilkey's first name as "Dav" instead of "Dave," he decides to adopt the new spelling.

1984 Pilkey enters Kent State University as an art major.

1986 Pilkey enters and wins the National Written and Illustrated by . . . contest. His entry, *World War Won,* is his first attempt at writing a children's book.

1987 Landmark Editions publishes *World War Won.* Pilkey embarks on his first author's tour, visiting schools and bookstores to publicize his book. Pilkey graduates from Kent State University with an associate of arts degree.

1990 *'Twas the Night before Thanksgiving* is published.

1991 The first title in the Dragon series, *A Friend for Dragon*, is published.

1993 Pilkey and his beloved dog, Little Dog, move from Ohio to Oregon; *Kat Kong* and *Dogzilla* are published.

1994 The first title in the Dumb Bunnies series, *The Dumb Bunnies*, is published.

1996 *The Paperboy*, Pilkey's first "serious" children's book, is published to widespread critical acclaim.

1997 *The Paperboy* is named a Caldecott Honor Book; *Big Dog and Little Dog*, the first in a six-book series, is published. *The Adventures of Captain Underpants: An Epic Novel* is published. The Captain Underpants series of books, now totaling eight volumes, is Pilkey's most popular to date and solidifies his position as one of America's favorite writers of books for young readers; Pilkey and Little Dog move from Oregon to a small island in Washington State.

2000 *Ricky Ricotta's Mighty Robot: An Epic Novel*, the first in a series of seven books, is published.

2005 Pilkey marries his longtime girlfriend, Sayuri, in a nighttime beach ceremony.

2006 *Captain Underpants and the Preposterous Plight of the Purple Potty People* is published.

NOTES

Chapter 1

1 National Public Radio, "Interview: Dav Pilkey Discusses His 'Captain Underpants' Books,"(September 20, 2003), http://www.highbeam.com/doc/1P1-85694632.html.

2 Ibid.

3 Sara Kelly Johns, "Speakout: Should Schools Promote 'Captain Underpants' Books?" *American Teacher* (April 2008), http://www.aft.org/pubs-reports/american_teacher/apr08/speakout.htm.

4 Ibid.

5 Ibid.

Chapter 2

1 Dav Pilkey, "The Almost Completely True Adventures of Dav Pilkey," http://www.pilkey.com/adv-text.php.

2 Kim Watts, "Interview with Dav Pilkey," *ADDitude Magazine* (September 2007), http://www.pilkey.com/int1.php.

3 Reading is Fundamental, "Interview with Dav Pilkey," *Reading Planet Book Zone*, http://www.rif.org/readingplanet/bookzone/content/pilkey.mspx.

4 Ibid.

5 Greater Dayton Public Television, "Dav Pilkey Biography," *Ohio Reading Road Trip* (2004), http://www.orrt.org/pilkey/.

6 Chris Duffy, "Interview with Dav Pilkey," *Nickelodeon Magazine* (September 1999), http://www.pilkey.com/int5.php.

7 Reading is Fundamental, "Interview with Dav Pilkey."

8 Kim Watts, "Interview with Dav Pilkey."

9 Reading is Fundamental, "Interview with Dav Pilkey."

10 Dav Pilkey, "The Almost Completely True Adventures of Dav Pilkey."

Chapter 3

1 Dav Pilkey, "Dav's Books: *World War Won*," http://www.pilkey.com/bookview.php?id=41.

2 Dav Pilkey, "The Almost Completely True Adventures of Dav Pilkey."

3 "Reader Review of *World War Won*," http://www.amazon.com/World-War-Won-Dav-Pilkey/dp/0933849222/ref=sr_1_1?ie=UTF8&s=books&qid=1256612460&sr=8-1.

4 Susan Scheps, "Review of *World War Won*," *School Library Journal* (1988), http://www.amazon.com/World-War-Won-Dav-Pilkey/dp/0933849222/ref=sr_1_1?ie=UTF8&s=books&qid=1256612460&sr=8-1.

Chapter 4

1 Answers.com, "Biography of Dav Pilkey," http://www.answers.com/topic/dav-pilkey-children-s-author.

2 Dav Pilkey, "Dav's Books: *'Twas the Night Before Thanksgiving*," http://www.pilkey.com/bookview.php?id=10.

3 "Review of *'Twas the Night Before Thanksgiving*," *Publishers Weekly* (1990), http://www.amazon.com/'Twas-Night-Before-Thanksgiving-Bookshelf/dp/0439669375/ref=sr_1_?ie=UTF8&qid=1231964502&sr=1-1.

4 Dav Pilkey, "Dav's Books: *Dragon's Merry Christmas*," http://www.pilkey.com/bookview.php?id=5.

5 Ibid.

Chapter 5

1 Dav Pilkey, "The Almost Completely True Adventures of Dav Pilkey."

2 "Review of *Kat Kong*," *Publishers Weekly* (1993), http://www.amazon.com/Kat-Kong-Dav-Pilkey/dp/0152049509/ref=sr_1_1?ie=UTF8&s=books&qid=1231965122&sr=1-1.

3 Dav Pilkey, "Dav's Books: *The Dumb Bunnies*," http://www.pilkey.com/bookview.php?id=23.

4 Answers.com, "Biography of Dav Pilkey."

5 Ibid.

6 Dave Pilkey, "Meet Sue Denim," http://www.pilkey.com/suedenim2.php.

Chapter 6

1 Dav Pilkey, "Dav's Books: *The Paperboy*," http://www.pilkey.com/bookview.php?id=11.

2 "Review of *The Paperboy*," *Publishers Weekly* (1996), http://www.amazon.com/Paperboy-Dav-Pilkey/dp/0531071391/ref=sr_1_1?ie=UTF8&=books&qid=1231965866&sr=1-1.

3 Answers.com, "Biography of Dav Pilkey."

4 Carolyn Phelan, "Review of *The Paperboy*," *Booklist*, http://www.amazon.com/gp/product/product-description/0531071391/ref=dp_proddesc_0?ie=283155&s=books.

5 American Library Association, "About the Caldecott Award," http://www.ala.org/ala/mgrps/divs/alsc/awardsgrants/bookmedia/caldecottmedal/aboutcaldecott/aboutcaldecott.cfm.

6 Answers.com, "Biography of Dav Pilkey."

7 Ibid.

8 Ibid.

9 Dav Pilkey, "The Almost Completely True Adventures of Dav Pilkey," http://www.pilkey.com/advtext.php.

10 Answers.com, "Biography of Dav Pilkey."

Chapter 7

1 Answers.com, "Biography of Dav Pilkey."

2 Ibid.

3 Ibid.

4 Ibid.

5 Beth Nissen, "Captain Underpants: The Straight Poop on a Grossly Entertaining Series of Children's Books," CNN.com (July 11, 2000), http://archives.com/cnn.com/2000/books/news/07/11/captain.underpants/.

6 Ibid.

7 Ibid.

8 Beth Nissen, "Interview with Dav Pilkey."

9 Gale Reference Team, "Biography—Pilkey, Dav," *Contemporary Authors Online* (2006).

10 Ibid.

11 Answers.com, "Biography of Dav Pilkey."

12 Ibid.

13 Ibid.

14 Kristina Asuwerwein, "Panel Torn over Fate of 'Super Diaper Baby,'" *Los Angeles Times* (June 5, 2003), http://articles.latimes.com/2003/jun/05/local/me-diaper5.

15 Ibid.

16 Ibid.

17 Dav Pilkey, "Dav's Response to the Controversy over Super Diaper Baby," http://www.pilkey.com/bookview.php?id=33.

Chapter 8

1 Dav Pilkey, "Dav's Books: *Ricky Ricotta's Mighty Robot*," http://www.pilkey.com/bookview.php?id=20.

2 Ibid.

3 Ibid.

4 Answers.com, "Biography of Dav Pilkey."

5 Dav Pilkey, "The Almost Completely True Adventures of Dav Pilkey."

WORKS BY DAV PILKEY

1987 *World War Won*

1988 *Don't Pop Your Cork on Mondays!: The Children's Anti-Stress Book* (as illustrator)

1990 *'Twas the Night Before Thanksgiving*

1991 *A Friend for Dragon*; *Dragon Gets By*; *Dragon's Merry Christmas*; *The Place Where Nobody Stopped* (as illustrator)

1992 *When Cats Dream*; *Dragon's Fat Cat*

1993 *Kat Kong*; *Dogzilla*; *Dragon's Halloween*; *Julius* (as illustrator)

1994 *The Dumb Bunnies* (written as Sue Denim); *Dog Breath!: The Horrible Terrible Trouble with Hally Tosis*

1995 *The Dumb Bunnies' Easter* (written as Sue Denim); *The Hallo-Wiener*; *The Moonglow Roll-O-Rama*

1996 *Make Way for Dumb Bunnies* (written as Sue Denim); *God Bless the Gargoyles*; *The Paperboy*

1997 *The Silly Gooses*; *The Dumb Bunnies Go to the Zoo* (written as Sue Denim); *The Adventures of Captain Underpants*; *Big Dog and Little Dog*; *Big Dog and Little Dog Getting in Trouble*; *Big Dog and Little Dog Going for a Walk*

1998 *The Silly Gooses Build a House*; *'Twas the Night Before Christmas 2: The Wrath of Mrs. Claus*; *Big Dog and Little Dog Wearing Sweaters*; *Big Dog and Little Dog Guarding the Picnic*

1999 *Captain Underpants and the Attack of the Talking Toilets*; *Captain Underpants and the Invasion of the Incredibly Naughty Cafeteria Ladies from Outer Space*; *Big Dog and Little Dog Making a Mistake*

2000 *Captain Underpants and the Perilous Plot of Professor Poopypants*; *Ricky Ricotta's Mighty Robot: An Epic Novel*; *Ricky Ricotta's Mighty Robot vs. the Mutant Mosquitoes from Mercury*

2001 *Captain Underpants and the Wrath of the Wicked Wedgie Woman*; *Ricky Ricotta's Mighty Robot vs. the Voodoo Vultures from Venus*; *The Captain Underpants Extra Crunchy Book O' Fun*

2002 *The Adventures of Super Diaper Baby: The First Graphic Novel*; *Ricky Ricotta's Mighty Robot vs. the Mecha Monkeys from Mars*; *Ricky Ricotta's Mighty Robot vs. the Jurassic Jackrabbits from Jupiter*; *The All New Captain Underpants Extra Crunchy Book O' Fun 2*

2003 *Captain Underpants and the Big, Bad Battle of the Bionic Booger Boy, Part 1: The Night of the Nasty Nostril Nuggets*; *Captain Underpants and the Big, Bad Battle of the Bionic Booger Boy, Part 2: Revenge of the Ridiculous Robo-Boogers*; *Ricky Ricotta's Mighty Robot vs. the Stupid Stinkbugs from Saturn*; *The Complete Adventures of Big Dog and Little Dog*

2005 *Ricky Ricotta's Mighty Robot vs. the Uranium Unicorns from Uranus*

2006 *Captain Underpants and the Preposterous Plight of the Purple Potty People*

POPULAR BOOKS

THE ADVENTURES OF CAPTAIN UNDERPANTS

This is the book that introduced the underwear-clad superhero Captain Underpants to a world of young readers. School pranksters George Beard and Harold Hutchins hypnotize cranky Principal Krupp with a 3-D Hypno-Ring. Krupp becomes Captain Underpants, determined to fight for truth, justice, and all that is pre-shrunk and cottony.

BIG DOG AND LITTLE DOG

Based on Pilkey's own "Little Dog" and the dog that lived down the street, Martha Jane, this was the first in a series of six books written for toddlers. Using minimal text and large illustrations, this volume shows the very youngest readers what dogs do best: sleep, eat, and act silly!

THE DUMB BUNNIES

First published under the pseudonym Sue Denim, *The Dumb Bunnies* salutes Harry Allard and James Marshall, the creators of The Stupids. Written in a deadpan style and illustrated with brightly colored cartoons, the series features a family of empty-headed bunnies who stumble their way through life. As it says on the cover of each of the books in the series, "This book is too dumb to win an award."

A FRIEND FOR DRAGON

This is the first in a series of five books about a gentle, lonely dragon. In this book a snake tricks Dragon into believing that an apple is his friend. Dragon is crushed when a hungry walrus eats the apple. Dragon buries the remains of the apple and is pleasantly surprised when a tree grows and provides him with a whole new crop of friends.

THE PAPERBOY

Dav Pilkey's award-winning (Caldecott Honor Book) book tells the simple tale of a young paperboy, his dog, and the magic of delivering newspapers in the still, quiet morning.

RICKY RICOTTA'S MIGHTY ROBOT

In this first book in the series, readers are introduced to a lonely little mouse named Ricky Ricotta who makes friends with a giant robot, takes on the school's bullies, and saves the city of Squeakyville from the evil rat scientist, Dr. Stinky McNasty.

POPULAR CHARACTERS

CAPTAIN UNDERPANTS

After being hypnotized by George Beard and Harold Hutchins with a 3-D Hypno-Ring, school principal Mr. Krupp becomes superhero Captain Underpants whenever he hears someone snap their fingers. Dressed only in underwear and a red cape, Captain Underpants saves the day fighting a variety of evildoers, including talking toilets, cafeteria ladies from outer space, the bionic booger boy, the wicked wedgie woman, and Professor Poopypants.

GEORGE BEARD AND HAROLD HUTCHINS

George, with a flattop haircut and tie, and Harold with a T-shirt and bad haircut, are the "creators" of Captain Underpants. The two are inseparable best friends. They both have a silly streak that constantly gets them into trouble. They also created Super Diaper Baby.

RICKY RICOTTA

Ricky is a gentle, mild-mannered mouse, who, with the assistance of his friend the giant robot, helps save Squeakyville from an assortment of nasty villains, including Mutant Mosquitoes from Mercury, Voodoo Vultures from Venus, Mecha Monkeys from Mars, Jurassic Jackrabbits from Jupiter, Stupid Stinkbugs from Saturn, and Uranium Unicorns from Uranus.

MAJOR AWARDS

1997 *The Paperboy* is selected as a Caldecott Honor Book.

1998 *Dog Breath* was awarded the California Young Reader Medal for primary readers.

BIBLIOGRAPHY

American Library Association. "About the Caldecott Medal." Chicago: American Library Association. 2009. Available online. URL: http://www.ala.org/ala/mgrps/divs/alsc/awardsgrants/bookmedia/caldecottmedal/aboutcaldecott/aboutcaldecott/cfm.

Answers.com. "Biography of Dav Pilkey." Answers Corporation, 2006. Available online. URL: http://www.answers.com/topic/dav-pilkey-children-s-author.

Askins, Gary D. "Don't Confuse Popular with Preferred," *American Teacher* (April 2008). Available online. URL: http://www.aft.org/pubs-reports/american_teacher/apr08/speakout.htm.

Davenport Public Library. "Banned—'Captain Underpants' by Dav Pilkey." Davenport, Ia.: DPL Kids Blog. Available online. URL: http://blogs.davenportlibrary.com/kids/?p=403.

Duffy, Chris. "Interview with Dav Pilkey." *Nickelodeon Magazine* (September 1999). Available online. URL: http://www.pilkey.com/int5.php.

Gale Reference Team. "Pilkey, Dav (1966–)" *Contemporary Authors*, Farmington Hills, Mich.: Gale, 2006.

Harrison, Dena. "A Scientific Mishap: Organizing a Story with Purposeful Paragraphs." Reno, Nev.: Northern Nevada Writing Project, 2009. Available online. URL: http://www.writingfix.com/Picture_Book_Prompts/Dogzilla3.htm.

Hatty, Michele. "Interview with Dav Pilkey," *USA Weekend*. Available online. URL: http://www.pilkey.com/int2.php.

Heller, Karen. "His Books Let Him Stay Class Clown, Even at 34." *Philadelphia Inquirer* (April 26, 2000).

Johns, Sara Kelly. "It's a 'Boy Thing'—and a Good One at That." *American Teacher* (April 2008). Available online. URL: http://www.aft.org/pubs-reports/american_teacher/apr08/speakout.htm.

Kennedy, Rose. "An Interview with Dav Pilkey." *Disney Adventures*. Available online. URL: http://www.pilkey.com/int4.php.

Kidsreads.com. "Biography of Dav Pilkey." New York: The Book Report, 2009. Available online. URL: http://www.kidsreads.com/authors/au-pilkey-dav.asp.

Ludden, Jennifer. "Interview: Dav Pilkey Discusses his 'Captain Underpants' Books." National Public Radio Weekend Edition, September 20, 2003. Available online. URL: http://www.highbeam.com/doc/1P1-85694632.html.

National Institute of Mental Health. "Attention Deficit Hyperactivity Disorder (ADHD)?" Washington, D.C.: National Institute of Mental Health, 2009. Available online. URL: http://www.nimh.nih.gov/health/publications/attention-deficit-hyperactivity-disorder/index.shtml.

Nick Mag Blog. "Q&A With Dav Pilkey." Nickonline, 2008. Available online. URL: http://www.nick.com/upickdaily/more/davpilkey-blogpost.jhtml.

Nissen, Beth. "An Interview with Dav Pilkey." CNN.com, July 11, 2000. Available online. URL: http://edition.cnn.com/2000/books/news/07/11/captain.underpants/transcript.html.

———. "Captain Underpants: The Straight Poop on a Grossly Entertaining Series of Children's Books." CNN.com, July 11, 2000. Available online. URL: http://edition.cnn.com/2000/books/news/07/11/captain.underpants/transcript.html.

Ohio Reading Road Trip. "Biography of Dav Pilkey." Dayton, Ohio: Think-TV, 2004. Available online. URL: http://www.orrt.org/pilkey/.

Paulson, Kenneth A. "Book-Burning In America: When Wizards Go Up in Smoke." freedomforum.org, January 13, 2002. Available online. URL: http://www.freedomforum.org/templates/document.asp?documentID=15610.

Phelan, Carolyn. "Review of *The Paperboy.*" *Booklist*. Available online. URL: http://www.amazon.com/gp/product/product-description/0531071391/ref=dp_proddesc_o?ie=283155&s=books.

Pilkey, Dav. *Dav Pilkey's Extra Crunch Website O' Fun*. Available online. URL: http://www.pilkey.com.

Ramsey, Inez, and Herb Wilburn. "Biography of Cynthia Rylant," Falcon.com. Available online. URL: http://falcon.jmu-edu/~ramseyil/rylant.htm.

Reading Planet/Book Zone. "Meet the Authors and Illustrators: Dav Pilkey." Reading Is Fundamental, 2008. Available online. URL: http://www.rif.org/readingplanet/bookzone/content/pilkey.mspx.

"Review of *Kat Kong*," *Publishers Weekly*, Reed Business Information, Inc., 1993. Available online. URL: http://www.amazon.com/Kat-Kong-Dav-Pilkey/dp/0152049509/ref=sr_1_1?ie=UTF8&s=books&qid=1231965122&sr=1-1.

"Review of *The Paperboy*," *Publishers Weekly*, Reed Business Information, Inc., 1996. Available online. URL: http://www.amazon.com/Paperboy-Dav-Pilkey/dp/0531071391/ref=sr_1_1?ie=UTF8&=books&qid=1231965866&sr=1-1.

"Review of *'Twas the Night Before Thanksgiving*," *Publishers Weekly*, 1990. Available online. URL: http://www.amazon.com/'Twas-Night-Before-Thanksgiving-Bookshelf/dp/0439669375/ref=sr_1_/ie=UTF8&qid=123964502&sr=1-1.

Sauerwein, Kristina. "Panel Torn over Fate of 'Super Diaper Baby,'" *Los Angeles Times*, June 5, 2003. Available online. URL: http://articles/latimes.com/2003/jun/05/local/me-diaper5.

Scheps, Susan. "Review of *World War Won*," *School Library Journal*, 1988. Available online. URL: http://www.amazon.com/World-War-won-Dav-Pilkey/dp/09338499109/ref=sr_1_1?ie=UTF8&s=books&qid=1231963808&sr=1-1.

Scholastic Book Club. "Interview with Dav Pilkey." London: Scholastic Ltd., 2008. Available online. URL: http://mybooks.co.uk/clubs_content/1492.

Scholastic Kids. "Captain Underpants Grownups Guide: Meet Dav Pilkey." New York: Scholastic, Inc., 2009. Available online. URL: http://www.scholastic.com/captainunderpants/grownups/developmental.htm.

Watts, Kim. "Dav Pilkey's Captain Underpants: Saving the School Day for ADHD Kids," *ADDitude Magazine*, September 2007. Available online. URL: http://www.pilkey.com/int1.php.

FURTHER READING

Allard, Harry G., and James Marshall. *The Stupids Die*. Mooloolaba, Australia: Sandpiper, 1985.

Dendy, Chris A. Ziegler, and Alex Ziegler. *A Bird's-Eye View of Life with ADD and ADHD: Advice from Young Survivors*. Cedar Bluff, Ala.: Cherish the Children, 2003.

McDonnell, Patrick, Karen O'Connell, and Georgia Riley de Havenon. *Krazy Kat: The Comic Art of George Herriman*. New York: Harry N. Abrams, 2004.

Petersen, Christine. *Does Everyone Have ADHD?: A Teen's Guide to Diagnosis and Treatment*. New York: Children's Press, 2007.

Rylant, Cynthia. *But I'll Be Back Again*. New York: HarperCollins, 1993.

Shulevitz, Uri. *How to Write and Illustrate Children's Books*. New York: Watson-Guptil, 1997.

Web Sites

Dav Pilkey's Official Web Site
http://www.pilkey.com

kidSPEAK: Where Kids Speak Up for Free Speech!
http://www.kidspeakonline.org

PICTURE CREDITS

page:

10: Urbano Delvalle/Time & Life Images/Getty Images

15: © INTERFOTO/Alamy

18: Columbia Pictures/Photofest

24: © bilwissedition Ltd. & Co. KG/Alamy

30: © Bettmann/CORBIS

38: UA/Photofest

43: Paramount Pictures/Photofest

50: AIP/Photofest

55: RKO Radio Pictures Inc/Photofest

60: Digital Image © The Museum of Modern Art/Licensed by SCALA/Art Resource, NY

68: Hal Roach/Photofest

72: Scholastic Inc./AP Photo

82: CBS/Photofest

INDEX

ABOUT THE CONTRIBUTOR

DENNIS ABRAMS attended Antioch College, where he majored in English and communications. A voracious reader since the age of three, Dennis is a freelance restaurant reviewer and writer who has written numerous books for young readers, including biographies of Hamid Karzai, Barbara Park, Xerxes, Jay-Z, Hillary Rodham Clinton, Rachael Ray, and Nicolas Sarkozy for Chelsea House. He currently resides in Houston, Texas, with his partner of 21 years and their dog, a Basenji named Junie B.